THE WEALTH WITHIN

*Self-help through a System of
Relaxing Meditation*

Ainslie Meares

HILL OF CONTENT
Melbourne

First published 1978
by Hill of Content Publishing Company Pty Ltd
86 Bourke Street Melbourne 3000 Australia
Reprinted 1979, 1982, 1983, 1984, 1985, 1986, 1987, 1988, 1990, 1993
© Copyright Ainslie Meares 1978
Printed in Australia by
McPherson's Printing, Maryborough, Victoria
National Library of Australia
Cataloguing-in-Publication data

Meares, Ainslie Dixon, 1910–86
   The wealth within.

   ISBN 0 85572 086 7

   I. Meditation. I. Title.

131.32

CONTENTS

Summary   ix
Introduction   xi

PART ONE   *Mental Ataraxis*

1 The Effects of Mental Ataraxis   3
2 The Relaxation of the Body   6
3 Experiencing the Relaxation   17
4 The Relaxation of the Mind   21
5 Our Posture For Mental Ataraxis   33
6 Meditating in Discomfort   48
7 Mental Ataraxis in Everyday Life   52

PART TWO   *The Discipline of Ease*

8   What We Do and What We Are   67
9   Our Life at Work   74
10 Our Life at Home   94
11 Our Sex Life   108
12 Our Leisure Life   115
13 Stress in Our Life   131

PART THREE   *The More Distant Horizon*

14 The Theoretical Basis of Mental Ataraxis   139
15 Beyond Relaxation   145
Epilogue   161

SUMMARY

Just for a moment let me summarise what I am going to talk about. You will then have a glimpse of the big picture, and the details which I shall describe will be seen in better perspective.

The theme is simple. It is a way to a better life. It will help us to understand each other if you can feel that I believe deeply both in the truth and in the importance of what we are about to discuss.

In the first place, anxiety does more than anything else at all to impair the quality of our life. We experience it as nervous tension and the unpleasant feeling of apprehension. It is anxiety which causes all our psychosomatic discomforts and disabilities. It causes the nasty feelings in our stomach and heart when we do not cope with stress situations. It causes our ulcers and predisposes our blood pressure troubles and our coronary heart attacks. It precipitates our asthma and headaches. Anxiety disturbs our bowels and menstrual function. It spoils our sleep. All this results from anxiety; but what I believe to be even more important is the fact that anxiety provokes us into defensive attitudes such as aggression, timidity, suspicion, greed and selfishness, and so makes us a lesser person than we might have been. Of course, anxiety also increases our perception of pain. If we have some chronic condition, the pain of it is so much the worse if we are tense. Life is better for us if we have a lower level of anxiety. Our mind has an inbuilt capacity to reduce the level of our anxiety; but our mind cannot exercise this capacity unless the circumstances are suitable. This is the essence of what I wish to discuss with you.

How do we provide the necessary conditions for our mind to use its natural ability to reduce anxiety? This is similar to the way in which our body can only exercise its capacity to repair physical injury if we provide suitable circumstances. In the case of a severe fever, we need rest. In the case of a fracture, it is a matter of immobilising the fragments of bone in their correct position. In the case of anxiety it is a matter of allowing the mind to come to a state of quiet and stillness.

By the very simple system of meditation which has come to be known as Mental Ataraxis we can let calm and stillness come to our mind so that anxiety is allayed.

Mental Ataraxis is a procedure which almost everyone can learn without much difficulty and without the expenditure of too much time. Ten minutes twice a day is usually sufficient for most people. In fact, the time spent on it is more than repaid by our increased ability to do things when we are more at ease in ourselves. The practice of Mental Ataraxis does not involve any withdrawal from active business life, and business men and women who practise it consistently report that they do more with less effort.

There are three important steps in learning Mental Ataraxis. The first is very simple. It is to learn complete, physical relaxation of the body. In the second step we learn to experience the relaxation of our body in our whole being so that our mind fully participates in it. The third step is very important. It is the experience of this relaxation in the face of minor discomfort. We sit, or squat, or lie down in such a posture that we are just slightly uncomfortable. Then we let ourselves relax and we are no longer aware of any feeling of discomfort. We practise this, and of course the only thing that really counts is the way in which we let the effects of it come into our daily life.

In the second part of the book I shall discuss with you how the discipline and the ease of Mental Ataraxis comes into the life we lead. We shall discuss this in relation to the different phases of our life – our life at work, our leisure life, our life at home, our sex life, our life when stress comes into it and our life in the changing circumstances of the world around us. With the simple, natural and effortless training of our mind in Mental Ataraxis we come to experience all these aspects of our life in the discipline of ease – and life is better for us.

INTRODUCTION

I think I shall feel more comfortable in myself if I commence by explaining that, over a period of more than thirty years of practice as a psychiatrist, I have been moving further and further away from the orthodox technology of psychiatry into the greater way of helping people by showing them how to manage their own state of mind through a variety of relaxing meditative experience. Over the last few years, besides seeing private patients, I have been showing people how to let their mind work in this fashion in large public groups of fifty to sixty people at a time in a small lecture room which I keep for this purpose.

Letters come in every day explaining: 'Life is better.' 'I have lost the feeling of tension that had plagued me for years.' 'Aches and pains are so much less.' 'Sleep better.' 'Not getting asthma like I used to.' 'I have not had a migraine for months.' Other people write in a slightly different way. 'I see things differently.' 'I am getting more out of life.' 'We seem to love each other in a way we did not before.' 'Family life has changed beyond all expectation.' There is no doubt that the lives of these people *have* changed for the better, and they have been able to describe the change in simple terms. But the quality of life is something very subtle, and there are others who write simply saying that there has been a change in their life for the better; there are some things that cannot be described in words.

It is out of this experience that I talk to you about Mental Ataraxis and an approach to a better experience of life. You may well wonder why I coined the name 'Mental Ataraxis' when such expressions as 'mental relaxation' and 'meditation' are now meaningful to most people through common usage. I gradually came to realise that many people were confused by my use of these terms when, in fact, I was referring to something that is slightly, but significantly, different. The procedure which is discussed in this book is much more than mental relaxation and it has clear differences from meditative practice as described in the Yoga and Zen texts and by the practitioners of the more modern variants such as Transcendental Meditation.

For clarity I have coined the phrase *Mental Ataraxis. Taraxis*, taken from the Greek, means 'a disturbance', so 'ataraxis' simply means 'an absence of disturbance'. Mental Ataraxis concerns quiet of the mind and peace of mind.

There is another point. To my knowledge most of the classical texts and most of the modern books on meditation give extensive descriptions to matters peripheral to meditation, but none of them answer very clearly the basic questions, 'How do I learn to meditate?' 'How do I bring my mind into a state of meditation?' 'How do I quieten my mind?' These are questions that *need* to be answered and I believe that they are, in fact, answered clearly and simply in the experience of Mental Ataraxis.

There is one matter in particular about which I seek your patience and understanding. With Mental Ataraxis, as with meditation in general, we are dealing with functions of the mind which lie outside the framework of the logical processes of our intellect. These are perfectly normal functions of the mind, but in ordinary life we have little awareness of them. Inasmuch as they lie outside the logical system, it is very difficult to describe them to you effectively through the logical communication of my writing. However we can come to understand them quite well through experiencing, whereas logical study leads us nowhere. So what I shall do is this: I shall discuss with you logically, as best I can, *how* you can let yourself experience these things. Thus the final understanding comes of your own experience and not from the logical content of what I write.

PART ONE

Mental Ataraxis

A Simple System of Meditation
The Practical Ordering of Our Inner Life

I

THE EFFECTS OF MENTAL ATARAXIS

This is a practical book on self-help, so I shall be practical right from the very start. Mental Ataraxis is a simple form of relaxing meditative experience which almost anyone can learn. When we practise it a little, it produces certain effects upon us. In a way, I would have preferred not to have described these effects to you at all. I would rather like you to have had the experience of them unfolding themselves to you, just as it has been with me and with many others, as a wider experience of a better life. Such an approach works well for those who already have an inner desire for something better. I have learned that they will go along with what I say. But I am practical. I know that there are many among us who will not venture into something new unless they can see pretty clearly what they are going to get out of it. It is for this very practical reason that I shall start by discussing with you some of the effects that you can expect from a little practice of this simple procedure.

The most important effect of Mental Ataraxis is a reduction in the general level of our anxiety. In fact, the other effects are nearly all secondary to the reduction of anxiety. I must emphasise one point in particular. Many of us – probably most of us – have grown so accustomed to our anxiety that we have come to accept it as natural. As a result we live out our lives in the belief that we are quite normal in ourselves. It is only when we come to reduce the level of our anxiety that we realise that we have been living a second class experience of life when something very much better was in fact available for us.

I have seen the evidence for this many, many times. Patients are often referred to me on account of some bodily symptom associated with nervous tension. Maybe the patient has an ulcer. He comes to me for help with this practical problem. He has no thought of seeking a better way of life. Yet, when I have used Mental Ataraxis to help such a person with their ulcer or some other ailment, they have often told me that their whole experience of life has changed, that they now have an ease of mind which they had never dreamed possible; yet they are doing just as much work, or more, than previously.

It is simply a matter of allowing the natural processes of the mind to reduce our anxiety. There is just one problem. This can take place only when the right circumstances are provided. Mental Ataraxis is simply an effective method of producing the right circumstances for this natural process to operate effectively.

There is a reduction of nervous tension and apprehension. Most of us are aware of·some nervous tension, and we know that life would be better if we were more at ease in ourselves.

Sometimes it is a matter of being tense with the boss at work, or tense with people on a social occasion, or the tension may show itself simply as irritability with our marriage partner and children. Sometimes it comes to us as apprehension in which we have the vague feeling of expecting something bad to happen. We fear something, but we really do not know what it is. But because of this fear we are uncomfortably over-alert and restless in all that we do. With some of us, instead of showing itself as nervous tension or apprehension, the anxiety becomes associated with some particular situation and we develop a phobia. We come to fear such things as travelling in lifts or aeroplanes, being in high places or simply being too far away from home. In each case the symptom arises through anxiety and when we reduce our anxiety the trouble is relieved.

All psychosomatic symptoms are the result of anxiety and they are allayed when anxiety is reduced by Mental Ataraxis. This, of course, is the practical and very valid reason that many people have for reading this type of book and following the advice in it. There are three aspects to the relief of psychosomatic troubles that I would stress.

In the first place, this approach avoids all the hazards of taking drugs. I have seen so much of the ill effects of taking tranquillisers and antidepressant drugs that I know that these hazards are very real. It is extremely easy to become 'hooked', with such a degree of dependence on the drugs that it can become very difficult indeed to discontinue them. There is also the hazard of side effects, and, of course, the potential danger to the unborn child of a mother taking these drugs, especially in the early stages of pregnancy. Then there is the general dulling effect. Those who take these drugs lose their former alertness and spontaneity, and for them life loses something of its natural colour and vividness.

The second point that I would emphasise to you is that we do not need to know the cause of an illness in order to get over it.

This is something very important. In the last fifty years we
have become obsessed about finding out the cause of nervous
troubles by endless going back to the conflicts of our childhood.
Even when it is possible, finding out the cause does not relieve
a nervous illness any more than it does a physical illness. Relief
requires something else – another compass – and this is available
to us in Mental Ataraxis.

The third point that I would like to stress is this. Please do
not feel that I am over-stating the effects of the reduction of
our anxiety by Mental Ataraxis. The evidence of how well it
works is simply indisputable.

*The effects of the reduction of our anxiety penetrate into all aspects
of our life.* When we are anxious we are continuously using our
mind to try to control our tension. As we become more relaxed
this effort of mind is no longer necessary, we can give our full
attention to the matter in hand and thought processes become
so much the easier. We think more clearly. There is a similar
effect in our emotional life. Anxiety inhibits our emotions, and
as we become less anxious we experience our emotions more
freely, there is greater joy in life. Our capacity for love and
compassion is increased.

The sexual responses in both men and women become freer
and more complete. Anxiety makes us over-alert and our nervous
system over-reacts. With anxious men there is an over-reaction
of sexual response and they come too quickly, while the nervous
tension of the anxious woman makes her unable to relax and
her normal sexual response is inhibited.

When we are relaxed we can do more work with less effort.
This is because we are free from the inhibiting effects of anxiety.
When we are relaxed we do not over-react when frustrated.
Our aggressive responses, either in the form of anger or irritability, are not so easily aroused. We become natural, so that we
are at ease with our friends and with our contacts in the course
of our working life. Our creative capacity is enhanced as the
alerting effect of anxiety no longer makes us over-cautious in our
thinking and feeling. In fact life becomes progressively better for
us as we reduce our anxiety.

Please remember that these are practical realities within our
grasp, so I shall go straight ahead and discuss the means of
attaining them. There are the other effects, the more subtle
effects of Mental Ataraxis. We will examine these later, as it will
be easier for you to appreciate them when you have some first-
hand knowledge of the process itself.

2

THE RELAXATION OF THE BODY

Different authorities attempt to define meditation in rather different terms. It is customary to regard concentration as simply holding the mind on some particular topic, while meditation is regarded as the flow of thought around this topic and the mental examination of the topic from every possible aspect. When viewed this way the process of meditation involves a conscious act of the mind, and is necessarily associated with some particular subject. According to circumstances, the meditator may choose such topics as God, Jesus, Siva, Buddha, OM, love or compassion. In this classical concept, as a result of the mind flowing around all aspects of the topic, the meditator comes to new understanding.

For the purpose of our present discussion I view meditation from a slightly *different point of view*. I consider the essential feature of meditation to be the principle that our mind functions in a different way in meditation from the way it functions in normal consciousness. As I see it, as meditation progresses, the activity of our mind becomes increasingly simple in nature.

First of all its logical, critical activity is reduced until this finally ceases. Then the vividness of our perception is reduced, noises come to be heard as sounds with little or no meaning. As the process continues there is little or no thought, and little or no awareness of sounds or activity around us. The process continues, and stillness comes to us. It is in this state that the natural processes of our mind act freely to reduce our anxieties.

From this brief description you will see that my idea of meditation differs from that of the classical concept in both the progressive reduction of mental activity and in the absence of any specific topic as an object on which the mind is focused. It is a process of extreme simplicity and naturalness and, as it has these clear differences from the classical concept, I refer to it as Mental Ataraxis.

We are going to let our mind capture the natural ease of things by experiencing the relaxation of our body. When we have done this we go further, much further, but this is the essential initial step in what we are about to do. It is a matter of letting our mind learn through experiencing its own naturalness, ease and effort-lessness.

The relaxation of our body is merely a prelude to relaxing our mind. It is not a part of the meditative experience. It is only the door by which we enter, something through which we must pass. It opens the way to the relaxation of our mind and the inner experience which lies beyond.

It is best to make our first venture into Mental Ataraxis just sitting in an armchair. We must remember that Mental Ataraxis is a dynamic process which grows with us. We start in the armchair; but as soon as we have learned to do it in an armchair, we make a progression of moves to less comfortable situations until the ease of it finally becomes a function of our mind quite indepen-dent of our bodily relaxation.

The first step is to sit in our armchair, comfortable, but at the same time symmetrically. I must ask you, particularly those of you who have had some knowledge of meditation, to go along with me about the details, the importance of which may not be obvious to you until you have had some taste of the experience itself.

We sit in the chair comfortably. We do not just flop into the chair with our body slumped in any irregular position which may come to it. We sit comfortable, in complete comfort, but at the same time with our body in a position of symmetry. Our arms rest on the sides of the chair, our knees are bent with the soles of our feet on the floor, and our head rests comfortably on the back of the chair. We are completely comfortable but at the same time in a position of natural symmetry.

The symmetry of our position in the chair is important as it intro-duces from the very beginning the feeling of some control into the apparently paradoxical feeling of utter relaxation. This idea will develop as we proceed with our Mental Ataraxis so that we come to attain an ease of control, a kind of effortless discipline of our whole self. For the present we just relax very completely, easily and naturally, but at the same time maintain a symmetrical position without allowing our body to slump in the chair.

As an initial step towards the relaxation of our body we can contract some of our muscles and then feel them relax as we let them go. This accustoms our mind to the feeling of our muscles being relaxed. In ordinary life we are often aware of our muscles being tense, but we are not often aware of them being relaxed. I have also learned that a great number of people believe that their muscles are relaxed when, in fact, they are not. The purpose of contracting our muscles and then letting them relax is simply to educate our mind so that we come to know when, in fact, our muscles are completely relaxed.

It is easiest to begin the contracting. and letting go with large muscle groups rather than small individual muscles. Start with the muscles of the front part of the thigh. As you sit comfortably in the chair with your knees bent, let your right hand rest on your right thigh. Then quietly raise your foot an inch off the floor. With your right hand you will feel the contraction of the muscles. Let your foot rest on the floor again and with your hand you feel the thigh muscles let go. Repeat this a few times until it comes quite easily. Then remove your hand from your thigh and let it rest on the arm of the chair. Repeat the slight movement of your foot and you can still feel the contraction and relaxation of the thigh muscles without the help of your hand resting on them. In other words your mind is becoming more perceptive of muscular relaxation.

Now bring your muscles to contract and let go by thinking of the movement, but without any movement of your leg at all. At first just think to yourself that you are going to lift up your foot. Just think it, but don't do it; and you will notice that the muscles of your thigh contract. Then think to yourself that you are letting your foot rest on the floor and you can feel the thigh muscles relax. Do the same with other muscles. By thinking of the movement of pushing the front part of your foot into the floor you can feel the muscles of the calf of your leg contract. Then they relax as the thought of movement goes from your mind. Similarly with the abdominal muscles. As you sit in the chair it is easy to contract these muscles and then let them relax.

The final step in the contracting and letting go of the muscles is to bring the muscles to move in this way simply by act of mind without thinking of any movement of the body at all. This is the natural progress of what we are doing. We can bring our thigh muscles to contract. We are aware that the muscles move, but there is no movement of our leg. While the muscles are contracted we are aware of the contraction. Then we let them relax. We are again aware of the movement of the muscles, but, most importantly, we are aware that they are now relaxed. We practise this a few times until we get the feel of it and then we do the same with other muscle groups, the calf muscles, the biceps and the abdominal muscles.

Please don't think, 'I can relax all right, so I can skip all this.' The success of Mental Ataraxis – and it is a very great success – depends very much upon our attention to details. It is only by mastering the simple things first that we attain the ease and naturalness which allows us to achieve what we are seeking.

The contraction and relaxation of the muscles is merely a step in the education of our mind in the feeling of relaxation, and as soon as this is achieved it is to be abandoned. This is important. It is important for this reason. The contracting and relaxing of our muscles is far too mechanical to help in real meditative experience. But more important, it makes us keep our mind active. We have to be alert, and understand what we are doing, when we contract and let go different muscles. It keeps our mind functioning at a rational level, aware of the practical realities around us. In Mental Ataraxis we transcend this mode of mental functioning; so any continuation of this contracting and relaxing of our muscles will only impede our progress.

We must make a transition from contracting and relaxing our muscles to a global experience of physical relaxation. There is no more of the contracting and letting go of the muscles. We just sit comfortably in the chair, arms resting on the sides, head resting on the back of the chair, and our whole body is relaxed. Everything is now relaxed – everything. We are now able to achieve this because we have become truly aware of physical relaxation. Our global relaxation is made easier by our feeling the effects of relaxation. As the muscles around our shoulders relax the full weight of our arms comes to rest on the sides of the chair. By feeling the natural weight of our arms weighing down on the sides of the chair the relaxation of the muscles of our shoulders and arms becomes so much the more complete. Similarly we feel the weight of our legs on the floor. We feel the weight of our whole body sinking into the chair. There is the feeling of us ourselves sinking into the chair, so relaxed that we seem to be a part of the chair itself. The global relaxation of our muscles is a total experience. All our muscles. All through us. The totality of it all. We experience it as utter and complete. As we let it come we may experience ourselves as sinking into it, sinking into the relaxation, deeper and deeper, more and more completely. Enveloped by it, as a mist silently envelops us on a mountain. It is calm, it is cool, it is fresh and it is silent. We are relaxed completely. More than feeling it. Just being it.

Although our relaxation is global in that it involves our whole body, and is complete in that it involves total relaxation of the muscles, getting comfortable is in no way a part of the experience. Until we have learned to let this experience come to us, the beginner needs to be reasonably comfortable when practising it. Comfort brings relaxation. But Mental Ataraxis is quite distinct from the relaxation of being comfortable. The comfort of an easy chair makes it easier for the beginner to capture the global relaxation. As soon as he has learned to experience this, he should not only cease to practise in conditions of physical comfort, but should progress to attaining the same experience in circumstances of increasing discomfort.

Relaxation through physical comfort has no significant effect on our general nervous tension. We are rested, and in this superficial way we are helped, but that is all. The relaxation that comes from being comfortable does not relieve our psychosomatic aches and pains, and it does nothing towards leading us towards an easier state of mind. Yet, because it is easy and pleasant people turn to this approach. They buy comfortable chairs in which they can be more relaxed.

Some two weeks ago I saw a new patient for the first time. He was a successful business executive, but very tense. He was determined to be more relaxed, and his coming to see me was just one aspect of his overall plan. During our discussion he disclosed that he was having an extra compartment added to his swimming pool in which the water would be really hot and soothing and an aid to the easing of his mind. I explained that my own experience with my swimming pool had been quite the reverse. I had got into the way of allowing myself to float about quietly in very cold water in winter in a very relaxed state so that I would no longer be conscious of the cold. The idea that one can gain ease of mind simply through physical relaxation is just a common delusion of our times.

On the other hand, physical relaxation is a necessary prelude to something greater. We need to start our experience of physical relaxation in a position of comfort, but this can be overdone. For instance, if we just flop on a comfortable bed, we can attain a great degree of physical relaxation. But in this case the relaxation comes about as a result of nervous impulses from our arms and legs and other areas of our body reporting to our brain that they are comfortable.

This is not what we are seeking. We are aiming for a different kind of relaxation, something that comes from our mind itself and is not dependent upon nervous impulses from parts of the body which are themselves comfortable. Hence we start in an easy chair maintaining symmetry of our body, and the complete physical relaxation of lying flopped on our bed has no place at all in our progress to Mental Ataraxis.

Although our relaxation is global and complete, nevertheless there remains sufficient tone in certain muscles to maintain posture. We do not give way to our bodily relaxation so that we just slump in the armchair. Our head rests on the back of the chair, our arms on the sides of the chair and our feet on the floor. Our body, when supported by the back of the chair, is completely relaxed. So are our arms and our legs because there is no need of any muscle tone to maintain their position. These are, in fact, completely passive. But with our head resting on the back of the chair it is slightly different. We need to maintain just sufficient tone in the muscles of our neck to prevent our head flopping to one side or falling forward. When we have captured the experience, the maintenance of our head in an erect position comes quite naturally, effortlessly and without our awareness that we are, in fact, keeping it in this position.

There is no making ourselves relax. We cannot relax by act of will. The procedure is completely free from effort and striving. If we try to relax, the very act of trying prevents us gaining the state of mind which we are aiming to attain. When we strive to relax, our mind is immediately occupied with the practical reality of our body, and the experience of the calm of our inner being is quite impossible. So there must be no attempt at trying to make ourselves do it; no making ourselves relax.

We cannot bring about relaxation by act of will, but by act of will we bring ourselves to a situation in which relaxation comes. We use act of will to bring ourselves to the decision to relax in meditative experience. We use act of will to sit comfortably and naturally in a symmetrical position in an easy chair, and in whatever other ways we prepare ourselves for the experience. Then we abandon all trying, striving and attempts to use our will in what we are doing.

Our eyes close as the physical relaxation comes to us. They close as a part of the whole process. When the muscles of our eyelids are relaxed, our eyes close. Quite effortlessly. They close themselves. We do not have to think about it at all. They close slowly. There is a slow letting go, as with other muscles when they relax. Quite distinct from the quick closure when we shut our eyes voluntarily, or the almost instantaneous closure when we blink.

As we relax, our eyes close, but as we become more profoundly relaxed they open just a little so that the margins of the lids are no longer touching. This is merely the result of complete relaxation of the muscles of the eyelids. When they are fully relaxed, the lids are no longer completely closed, but open just slightly as this is their natural position when all the tone has gone from the muscles. We notice this as we become aware of a glimmer of light coming to our eyes, or we may even be aware of objects in our immediate line of vision. But with a little experience this awareness passes, and in the stillness of our mind we have only a vague sensation, either of light coming to our eyes, or objects in front of us.

Sometimes the beginner is disturbed by a fluttering of the eyelids. He feels them quiver and he cannot bring them to remain still. He becomes frustrated. The quivering eyelids command his attention, and stillness of the mind becomes impossible. This is merely an anxiety reaction to a new experience. We have a built-in protective reaction to keep our eyes open when we are doing something new. When we let ourselves relax we let our eyelids close, but the old protective reaction tries to keep them open, hence the fluttering. The problem soon disappears with a little practice.

People who are very anxious may at first have difficulty in letting their eyes close at all. This is merely the same protective reaction in more advanced form. If you should be troubled in this way, please do not abandon the meditative experience, as the difficulty in closing your eyes means that you have a very high level of anxiety, and the chances are that you will obtain great benefit from this type of experience. Don't force yourself to close your eyes. This only increases the level of anxiety. Just let them stay open. Then as the relaxation comes to your other muscles, particularly those in the face, you will find that your eyes close themselves without your worrying about it at all.

I have recently seen a woman with an extremely severe anxiety reaction. She had been living in a state of really excruciating apprehension. In ordinary circumstances she would have required hospital treatment. She was quite unable to let her eyes close even for a moment. If I let my fingers rest on her face to encourage the lids to close, it produced acute panic. However she overcame the difficulty when I brought her to hold her hands over her face when she started to relax. But troubles of this severity are extremely rare.

The relaxation of certain parts of our body is more important than others. The parts of our body which have a greater nerve supply are more significant than those parts which have less nerve supply.

Thus the face and hands are more important than the back. Also, those parts of our body which, in normal circumstances, are only partially under our control are more important than those over which we normally have fairly complete voluntary control. Thus the control of our muscles of facial expression is less complete than those of our arms and legs, and their relaxation is correspondingly more significant.

The relaxation of our face is very important. As we let our body relax we come to feel the relaxation in our face; then, as we become more expert, the relaxation is just there without our specifically feeling it at all. However, at the start it is a great help to consciously feel the muscles of our face relax. The tension goes from the cheeks. The muscles that move the jaw relax so that the jawbone itself sags a little. The lips are relaxed, and with the sagging of the jaw, the lips part just a little in a state of complete relaxation. The muscles of the forehead relax and the forehead itself is felt to smoothe out. This is most important as the smoothing out of the forehead has a stilling effect on the mind itself.

Our hands are also very important. As we relax, our hands take up a position of ease. The wrist is bent and the fingers flexed, the little finger rather more so than the index. As we sit in our chair it often happens that our hands protrude beyond the arms of the chair. When our hands are in this position our wrists are flexed so that our hands hang downwards of their own weight.

At the start, our awareness of our physical relaxation is very important, but, as we progress towards Mental Ataraxis, the need for this awareness passes. Once we have mastered the ability of complete relaxation our experiencing the awareness of it is no longer necessary. Our mind is then no longer encumbered with this awareness which can detract from the higher aspects of the complete experience. Something like this happens in driving a car; we perform without the distracting awareness of each action taken. This is just another example of the way in which the path to Mental Ataraxis is a progression of minor experiences. Each step in itself is important, but once we have made it, we leave it behind.

As we relax, we can experience the relaxation of the muscles of the perineum. These are the muscles down below between the bones of the pelvis which keep our lower organs in place. In normal conditions we are hardly aware of these muscles at all. When we first learn to contract and to let go our muscles we can do the same with the perineal muscles by consciously drawing the anus upwards and then letting it go down again from the weight of the organs above. But even when the contracting and letting go is not used, we still become aware of the relaxation of these muscles as part of the total relaxation of our whole body. The awareness of the relaxation of the perineal muscles comes about through the slight movement which occurs as they relax. With our arms and legs there is very little movement at all as they relax, but if we are in a sitting position and the tone goes from the perineal muscles, they sag a little due to the weight of the organs pressing on them. It is this slight movement which brings their relaxation into our awareness.

We do not examine ourselves to see whether we are relaxed or not. There can be no asking ourself, 'Am I properly relaxed?' If we do this we are using our minds in the alert critical fashion which we want to avoid in the meditative process. Afterwards, when we have stopped meditating, we can ask ourselves, 'Was I properly relaxed?' But we cannot put the question to ourselves while we are actually in the process of meditation. Furthermore, if we question ourselves in this fashion, we increase the level of our anxiety, and so increase the tension of our muscles. Instead of questioning ourselves, we just feel the relaxation, experiencing it naturally and completely.

As we relax, our breathing becomes deep and regular. When we assume our posture in preparation for relaxation we are in no way conscious of our breathing, as in our normal state of mind we are quite unaware of our breathing or any movement of our chest or diaphragm. However, in the stillness of relaxation, our breathing may intrude into our consciousness. Another factor contributes to this. In complete relaxation we let ourselves go off-guard. The beginner is a little nervous about this, and his anxiety may make him aware of his breathing. But as the relaxation becomes more complete, all awareness of our breathing is lost.

In Mental Ataraxis it is not necessary to concentrate on breathing. Certainly in concentrating on the breathing we experience the rhythm, the drawing in of the air, the holding, the letting out, the emptiness, then the drawing in again, and with it a sense of timelessness – a process that can make it easier for the beginner for it occupies his mind and so prevents frustration from the intrusion of irrelevant thoughts. To this extent it is helpful, but, at the same time, it detracts from the profound simplicity of the type of relaxing meditative experience which we are aiming to attain. Awareness of our breathing may become a very simple form of awareness, but it is still an awareness of practical reality, and in this way prevents the experience of the essential stillness of our being which comes to us as we achieve Mental Ataraxis.

In experiencing physical relaxation we allow our mind to go off-guard. This defencelessness may produce transient anxiety. Through countless generations we have become conditioned to keeping ourselves alert so that we are in a position to meet any possible danger. The letting go of our mind to experience physical relaxation runs contrary to this biological conditioning. So, as we begin to let go, our mind keeps bringing us back to be alert again, and the relaxing experience is temporarily interrupted. This is a simple automatic defence which is ingrained into us to save us from danger. As we continue the relaxing experience our mind comes to realise, as it were, that no harm comes from it, and these momentary interruptions gradually cease.

Some people relax quite well at first, but then become anxious, and freeze into a tense state while still retaining their outward appearance of relaxation. This is a simple anxiety reaction. If the beginner should become aware of tension developing in his muscles, he can often get through the difficult phase by consciously allowing the muscles to relax. If this fails, he may free himself of the tension by making a slight movement of his arms and legs. If this should also fail, he should stand up and have a rest for a few minutes. Then he can resume the relaxation, but on this occasion for only a very short time, perhaps for two minutes or even less. He should repeat these very short sessions in which there is not sufficient time for the tension state to develop. In this way he will accustom himself to the relaxing experience without the development of anxiety and consequent muscle tension. But these measures will rarely be necessary, as with most people the experience of relaxation comes quite easily and naturally.

What should I think about while my body is relaxing? Teachers of the traditional schools of meditation usually advise that the mind should be fixed on some focal point. The problem in this approach is that it is extremely difficult for the beginner to maintain concentration on a single topic without the mind wandering. Those who teach the modern variants of traditional meditation often recommend that the student should visualise some pleasant and relaxing scene such as a lakeside on a still day. This is much easier for the student as he can let his mind fill in various details of the scene.

Since this, in itself, is a distraction from the essential simplicity of Mental Ataraxis, I would advise you *not to think of anything*. If you continue to feel the relaxation of your body, the feeling process will, of itself, quieten your mind so that you are not worried by the intrusion of unwanted thoughts.

Does the repetition of a mantra help the relaxation? A mantra is a syllable or phrase which in itself is meaningless, but which is given to the student by the teacher as having some special meaning for the student. It is his secret syllable as it were. The meditating student keeps repeating the mantra softly to himself. Many classical forms of Yoga as well as modern Transcendental Meditation rely heavily on the repetition of mantras. This occupies the mind and so helps to avoid extraneous thoughts. Among other purposes, the monotony of constant repetition of mantras has a lulling effect on the intellect so that the logical, critical faculties are less active with the result that the transcendental functions of the mind are more likely to emerge. All this is to the good. But for the purpose of achieving successful Mental Ataraxis, I believe that the use of the mantra introduces too mysterious an element into something which can be achieved by very simple, completely natural methods.

3

EXPERIENCING THE RELAXATION

We have now learned how to let our body relax while sitting comfortably in our armchair. The next step is to experience this relaxation of our body.

Experiencing our physical relaxation is something quite different from being physically relaxed. It is the next step towards the stillness of mind which comes in Mental Ataraxis. I am an Australian, and in the summer months I see tens of thousands of my fellow Australians sunbathing on the beaches. They lie there, their burnished bodies drinking in the sunshine. With many of them, their bodies are relaxed; very completely so. They, themselves, feel drowsy, relaxed and easy. But they are not experiencing the relaxation of their body in the way that we must if we are to achieve Mental Ataraxis. This is something different. It is easy to understand it when you experience it, but it is a little difficult to explain in writing because we do not have any apt words or phrases to help us, so will you please go along with me about this?

Physical relaxation is merely a state of our body. The sunbathers achieve it, and most of us reach a state of physical relaxation in bed at night just before sleep comes to us. Many achieve it with the help of a good masseuse. We, ourselves, have learned to capture it sitting in our armchair. Now we must go further than this.

Experiencing the relaxation of our body is more than the awareness that we are relaxed. Nevertheless, this is a necessary step in the process. We have, in fact, prepared ourselves for this by experimenting with the contraction and letting go of our muscles. By this means we have become more aware of the state of our muscles. We have advanced from the contracting and relaxing of muscle groups to the global relaxation of our body. Through this we have gained some awareness of the state of relaxation of our body as a whole.

Awareness of our relaxation is a function of our intellect. It belongs to that order of mental activity by which we are aware of all the important, but at the same time mundane, aspects of practical reality which surround us. We must bring our mind to go beyond this way of working. In Mental Ataraxis, it is not so much that our mind does not perceive practical realities, but rather that it perceives these practical realities of life in such simple and harmonious fashion that the mundane aspect of practical reality is completely transcended.

However, our present task is to experience the relaxation of our body in a way that is beyond the intellectual awareness of our relaxation.

Feeling the relaxation of our body is a step towards experiencing it. Firstly we must distinguish between the two processes, awareness and feeling. One is a function of the intellect and the other concerns the sensory aspects of our mind.

Now, as we sit in our chair, let us feel the relaxation. No contracting and letting go of muscles. Just the feeling of it all. Our total relaxation. Global relaxation. It almost overcomes us. Our forehead is smoothed out with it. So relaxed, we seem to be sinking into the chair. The feeling of utter relaxation. Utter. But at the same time our head remains there, resting on the back of the chair without flopping sideways or slumping forwards. It is the feeling of the relaxation. Feeling it all the time.

As far as relaxation is concerned, we can easily be misled by both our awareness and our feeling. This is strange, but it is true. Almost every day some patient says something like this to me, 'But I am aware I am relaxed. I can feel that I am relaxed.' At the same time it is perfectly obvious to me, from moving the patient's arms, that he is in no way relaxed at all. Our awareness and our feeling are based in our past experiences of life. If we have been tense for years, as many of us have, there is no basis of previous experience on which to judge our awareness and feeling of relaxation. Of course, many such people do not know that they are living a very inferior experience of life which could be very greatly enhanced with a little guidance. For the present, we just want to be sure that our awareness and feeling of relaxation is based on reality.

We can test the reality of our awareness and feeling of relaxation by having some friend lift up our arm and let it go suddenly. We are sitting in our armchair relaxing with our arms resting on the arms of the chair. Our friend takes hold of our forearm and raises it two or three inches. Then he suddenly lets it go. If we are in fact relaxed our arm falls instantaneously and heavily. If we are not completely relaxed, the residual tension of the muscles prevents our arm falling as a dead weight. It falls more slowly than it should, and there may be a split second's delay from the time the arm is released before it actually falls. This of course is due to the fact that the muscle tension of nervous people tends to hold the limb in a fixed position. However, it is our friend himself who can readily let us know whether we are relaxed or not. He can tell by the weight of our arm as he lifts it up. An arm is really quite heavy. But if we are tense our muscles involuntarily help in lifting it up, and our friend loses the sense of heaviness of the limb.

In the absence of a friend we can test ourself in a similar fashion, although it is slightly more difficult. We let ourself relax as completely as we can. Then still retaining our relaxation we raise one arm by lifting it up by the other hand. The arm which we are lifting remains completely relaxed and passive. We become aware of the heaviness of the arm as we lift it up. Then we let it go suddenly and it falls with its dead weight. In doing this I have found that it is best to lift the arm with the index finger of the other hand under the cuff of the relaxed arm. We lift it up. Then we let our finger slip from the cuff. This ensures the sudden release of the arm so that any delay in its falling back is easily observed.

Our awareness of relaxation and the feeling of it are both necessary steps in experiencing relaxation, but once this is achieved our awareness and feeling of it should cease. Once again, this is another example of the way in which the path to Mental Ataraxis is a progression of simple experiences. Once the experience has fulfilled its purpose we abandon it for something better. We cannot take the step to the summit without the earlier steps up the slope. As long as we retain awareness of being relaxed, or the feeling of being relaxed, the greater experience of stillness will elude us.

We both feel the relaxation of our minds and feel relaxed in ourselves. These are two different experiences. We have learned to feel the relaxation of our muscles. This is the feeling, the sensation, of the physical relaxation of our body. From this we can take the next very important step of just feeling relaxed.

More than our body relaxes. Now it is our whole self that is relaxed, our ego, our total being. When we, ourselves, are

participating in it, we have moved a step closer to Mental
Ataraxis. It is no longer a matter of our muscles or our body
being relaxed because the distinction between our body and
ourself has faded. It is all one. The relaxation becomes a total
experience which involves our whole being.

*Experiencing our physical relaxation is more profound than being
aware of it or feeling it.* Being aware of our relaxation involves
two entities. There is ourself, or our ego, which is aware, and
then there is the relaxation of which we are aware. There are
the same two entities when we feel our relaxation. Ourself, which
does the feeling, and the thing we feel.

It would be easy to say that the same must apply when we
come to experiencing; we who experience and the thing experienced. This is where my use of words fails. The idea that I am
trying to communicate is that this duality is transcended in this
kind of experience which I am attempting to describe. The
separate entities cease to be separate. There is now only one.
The experience, ourself and the relaxation are all one.

4

THE RELAXATION OF THE MIND

Sitting in our chair we have mastered the physical relaxation of our body, and we have now come not only to be aware of our relaxation and to feel it, but to actually experience it as part of ourself so that it is an integral part of our being. The next step is the relaxation of our mind.

We may relax very completely, but at the same time fail to participate in it. The physical relaxation is genuine, but the mind remains alert. This state of affairs comes about through anxiety. We feel there is no danger in letting ourselves relax provided we can come out of it at a split second's notice. This of course prevents the development of Mental Ataraxis. In clinical practice this state is easily recognised when, at the end of a session, I tell the participants to open their eyes. Those who have been fully participating in the experience open their eyes quite slowly, whereas anyone who has relaxed physically, but has remained mentally alert opens his eyes immediately I give him the cue to do so.

The experience of our physical relaxation brings with it the relaxation of our mind. It does not come from the simple awareness that we are physically relaxed. When we are aware of our physical relaxation our mind has to stand apart, as it were, in order to attain the awareness of something else. But when we experience the relaxation there is no standing apart, and our mind itself participates in our bodily relaxation.

The relaxation of our mind is not just a matter of experiencing comfort from the relaxation of our body. With our body relaxed we have the feeling of comfort. We experience this in bed when we are about to go to sleep. Just before sleep comes our mind is, in fact, relaxed. But the type of relaxation of our mind which we seek is beyond this. The relaxation of our body, and the comfort which comes from it, is only an experience along the way into this greater, deeper and more complete form of mental relaxation. And when we have attained it, there is no need for either physical relaxation or comfort, as it is independent of both.

The relaxation of our mind is not due to drowsiness. At night, as sleep comes to us, we are aware of the drowsiness, and with it there is relaxation of our mind, and we merge into sleep. But in Mental Ataraxis our mind is profoundly relaxed, but not drowsy, not sleepy, not asleep, and in its complete form quite still and empty of thought.

The beginner sometimes feels that, if the mind is still and empty of thought, the individual must be either asleep or unconscious. This is not so. There is this other state. The deep relaxation of the meditating mind. The person who is unconscious has no awareness at all. In sleep we either have no awareness or the distorted awareness of dreams. In the mental relaxation of meditation, we experience the stillness of it. This experiencing is a very simple, primitive function of the mind which does not involve clear consciousness as in the case of awareness.

After their first attempt at relaxation people often say to me, 'I relaxed my body quite well, but I could not get it into my mind.' Of course some people expect too much, too quickly. Please don't let yourself fall into this error. Learning Mental Ataraxis is not a tedious business requiring months of practice. On the other hand it is unreasonable to expect dramatic changes at the first attempt.

There is another pitfall. To many people, the relaxation of the body comes very easily. This is good; but it is not good when they tend to skip the exercise of fully experiencing the relaxation because it all appears rather vague or they reason that it is perhaps unnecessary for them. Because of this they judge their first attempt on the degree of stillness that they can attain in their mind. They are trying to run before they can walk. Let us take things step by step and progress to Mental Ataraxis will be simple enough.

Our muscles do in fact relax, but when we talk of relaxation of our mind we are speaking figuratively. Physically there is less tension in a relaxed muscle fibre, but there is no analogous physical relaxation of the nerve cells of our brain. We experience anxiety as a feeling of tension. By relaxation of our mind we refer to the easing of this tension. In this it is well to remember that nearly everyone has a higher level of anxiety than need be, so almost all of us are capable of experiencing mental relaxation simply through a reduction in the general level of our anxiety. This, of course, is a feature of Mental Ataraxis.

Our mind participates with our body in total relaxation. This comes about through the *experiencing*; not through knowing that we are relaxed, feeling relaxed or being aware of it. Being it. And when this 'being it' comes to us, our mind is relaxed with our body because it is all part of the same process.

Some systems of meditation involve intense concentration of the mind, but in Mental Ataraxis there is utter effortlessness. No effort. No trying. No striving. No making ourself do it. No effort at all. No striving for effortlessness. No making ourself go with it. It is just there. Going with it in utter effortlessness. This is the experience of it. Very simple. Utterly easy. Something quite wonderful.

Real effortlessness is essential for Mental Ataraxis. Some people fall into the error of thinking about the effortlessness of what they are doing. Of course the very process of thought destroys the effortlessness of the experience. In thinking about it they are striving for it, and the act of striving negates the effortlessness. Please do not think that I am just bandying words with you. Let yourself experience it, and you will understand what I mean.

The effortlessness of the approach leads us into stillness of our mind. This basic truth would seem to be obvious. But it eludes many who teach meditation and who write on these matters. If we are striving for something, or if we are concentrating on something, there can be no real stillness of the mind, whereas the experience of effortlessness is the pathway to our mind by which stillness enters so easily.

The effortlessness of Mental Ataraxis initiates us into the discipline of ease. Our effortlessness becomes a learning experience of great significance to us. We learn to meditate without effort. In fact we learn to do something which could be difficult, and we learn to do it quite effortlessly. In this way the effortlessness of Mental Ataraxis becomes a prototype for other experiences in our every-day life. As a result of this experience we find that we manage other tasks with ease which would otherwise have been difficult.

The effortlessness of Mental Ataraxis is experienced as something quite wonderful. This is so because it opens up a new dimension of human experience which is almost completely unknown to most of us. Since early schooldays we have been educated to strive to attain what we desire. Our whole life has been striving.

But here we have something of great importance that is only obtainable without effort. An entirely different approach. And of course the same principle is applicable to so much of life. When our mind is running smoothly we just do the thing that has to be done, and there is no effort about it at all. So in Mental Ataraxis we come to experience something of the discipline of ease.

We cannot know that our mind has been relaxed until afterwards. We may find that we ask ourselves, 'Is my mind relaxed?' If this happens, of course it is not relaxed as the fact of enquiring about the state of our mind involves our critical faculties and so of necessity prevents relaxation. It is only when our meditative experience has come to an end, and we have again become aware of the realities around us, that we know that we have just emerged from a state of mental relaxation.

We must avoid examining our state of mind. As we first experience our physical relaxation, our mind fluctuates between moments of complete relaxation and moments of relative alertness. In the more alert moments we cannot help examining in retrospect the state of mental relaxation from which we have just emerged. The feeling comes to us, 'I must capture that again.' There is a tendency here to try to recapture it, and of course the trying prevents it coming. Effortless. We must always remember that it is effortless.

A similar fluctuation of mental state commonly occurs from one session to the next. A good session may be followed by one which is not so good. This usually results from the desire to repeat or surpass the success of the earlier session. The essential effortlessness is lost, and the individual starts to strive for it, and the experience eludes him.

The secret to the relaxing of our mind is the total experience of the relaxation of our body. It is the totality of the experience which is so important. It is not just the experience of our whole body being relaxed. More than our body it is our whole self.

When the relaxation includes every aspect of our being, then our mind itself participates in it. This of course is true, and we realise the truth of it as the experience comes to us. When everything is relaxed, our mind is relaxed too.

As we experience the relaxation of our body, we let the experience spread out, as it were, until it invades our total being – invades the whole of us. It now encompasses far more than our body. It comes as quietness, and an ease, pervading everything –

our thoughts, our feelings, our whole being. It all follows quite easily and naturally from experiencing the relaxation of our body. We just allow it to become more complete, totally complete. Thought ceases, we are beyond feeling, and our mind is relaxed like the rest of ourself.

We attain relaxation of our mind by letting ourself go with the relaxation of our body. It is a matter of letting ourself participate with complete freedom in the experience of relaxation. There is ease and naturalness in this letting go. Letting go freely. We let ourselves go further than the relaxation of our body, we let ourselves relax in our whole being, and it is in our mind. All the time there is this easy, natural experience of letting ourself go with the relaxation without restraint. Effortlessly.

We let ourselves experience the essential calm of our being. Again it is a letting go. We are aware of the natural calm deep within us. We let ourselves experience it. Naturally. It is all natural. We let the calm of it come all through us. And as we do so, we experience the relaxation of our mind.

The experience of calm is felt differently by people: '...a calm without trying.' 'It was terrific...still conscious, but completely relaxed.' 'A calm of mind I've never felt before.' 'It was like *finding* some sort of calm...some pool of calm.' '...a calm that has reminded with me.' 'Calm within myself.' 'I feel so much calmer, it's incredible!'

At first the relaxation of our mind waxes and wanes. This is what we would expect. There are moments of completeness and moments in which the experience is less complete. Moments of stillness may be interrupted by moments of full alertness. Do not be disturbed by these fluctuations. With practice the phases of stillness become longer and longer, and these fluctuations in the completeness of the experience become less and less.

At the start, the relaxation of our mind may be interrupted by a sudden feeling of panic. If this should happen do not be alarmed by it. This is simply a transient anxiety reaction. For self protection our mind has become trained to remain on the alert. When our mind first relaxes, we may suddenly become aware that we are unguarded, and awareness of possible danger through lack of alertness brings the sudden panic which has the protective value of immediately bringing us to full consciousness. If this type of reaction should come to you, just quietly continue with your practice in the knowledge that the trouble will soon cease as your mind becomes accustomed to the experience of complete relaxation.

We brought the relaxation of our body into our mind by experiencing it, now we can intensify the process by letting ourselves experience the natural calm within us. From talking of such matters with patients it has become clear to me that there are many among us who are scarcely aware of the natural calm within us. Many are quite unfamiliar with the experience of complete physical relaxation of body. The experience is a pleasant discovery for them and they are delighted to have been able to fully experience it. *Now* is the time for this other, this more complete, experience. *But this is not of the body, it is of the mind.*

The natural calm within us is to be distinguished from the calm of drowsiness. It is the ease of the smooth functioning of our body and our mind. Expressed like this it sounds rather pedestrian. This is so only because so few of us ever experience the smooth functioning of our body and mind. When it comes to us it is really an experience of the highest order. Something that far transcends the ordinary experience of life as most of us know it. People whom I have been leading into Mental Ataraxis have often said to me, 'That was wonderful, truly wonderful.' From the expression of their face I have known that what they said was true, and that for the first time in their lives they had experienced the natural calm within us.

We become aware of the natural calm within us when our mind is completely free from anxiety. This, of course, comes to us in Mental Ataraxis. It is analogous to the feeling of calm in our body when we first experience the complete absence of tension in our muscles. But the calm within us is not of the body, it is of the mind, and the experience is so much the more complete.

The calm within us comes as anxiety ebbs from us, but the process can be facilitated by letting ourselves anticipate what we are about to experience. All the time we have the general attitude of mind of letting ourselves go with the experience of Mental Ataraxis as it comes to us. At different times the letting go can apply more particularly in certain areas. Thus, at the start, we feel the letting go particularly in relation to our body and the muscles of our body. All the time we let ourselves go with the process in which we are participating. Now we let ourselves feel the calm within us. We let ourselves experience it deeply, all through us. Our letting go intensifies the process, and the calm within us becomes a reality.

We experience the relaxation of our body, and we experience the relaxation of our mind, but it is more, it is our whole being. As we let ourself go with it the boundaries of body and mind disintegrate. We let go still more completely and a greater experience of unity comes to us. It is our being, our whole being of which our body and our mind are merely different facets. We come to experience the relaxation of our body and of our mind as the calm and ease of our whole being. And all the time there is the letting ourself go with it, so that the experience is both deep and high, as well as intense and real.

In Mental Ataraxis we let ourselves be. Of all human activity, of both body and mind, this is the simplest and the most primitive – the act of just being in all its simplicity and naturalness with nothing added at all; not even being alive, as this involves our awareness. It is the unadorned, primordial experience of existence. This is *simple being.* Of course, inaminate objects have being, but they cannot experience their state; but when *we* experience simple being we share something of all that is around us, far and near. Sometimes the experience of simple being comes to us in moments of reverie, sometimes when we are very relaxed, sometimes when sleep is almost upon us. If we think about our being, the simplicity of the experience is lost, we are thinking, and pure being has eluded us.

Pure being is a defenceless state, and unconscious protective reactions intervene to prevent us exposing ourselves to the potential danger of defencelessness. When we first attempt to just let ourselves be, we often find that against our conscious wish there is something keeping us alert. This is a manifestation of an unconscious protective reaction. It may show itself in various forms. Our mind may become unusually active so that all manner of thoughts come to us. On the other hand, we may find ourselves unduly restless. We do not seem to be comfortable, although there is clearly no reason why we should not be comfortable. The restlessness, of course, keeps us alert and so protects us from the imagined danger of the defencelessness of simple being. We must remember that in the circumstances of our meditation the danger of simple being is imagined, but in other aspects of life any tendency to lapse into unguardedness may, in fact, be dangerous as we would become exposed to the risk of danger from both our physical environment and our fellows.

The less anxious we are, the easier it is to let ourselves be. This is so because anxiety alerts all our protective reactions. So all those things which work to reduce our anxiety will help us to let ourselves experience our simple being.

Just as the stillness of meditation is coming to him, the beginner may be suddenly brought back to material reality by a sudden jerk of his whole body. This is a protective reaction. When we have been tense for a long time we become accustomed to holding on to ourselves, as it were. Keeping a grip of ourselves. We do this unconsciously to guard against the threat of psychological disintegration which anxiety brings with it. Then we let go in the meditative process. We are no longer holding on to ourselves, or keeping a grip of ourselves. Our mind suddenly feels that we are in danger, and the sudden jerk of our body is a protective reaction to put us on guard again.

This sudden jerk of the body is not very common, but it may be quite frightening. If it happens to you, remember that no harm comes of it. If you practise a few times, your mind learns by experience that there is no danger in letting yourself go off-guard, and the reaction ceases.

Sometimes the beginner may be disturbed by a sudden feeling of acute panic just when the stillness of the mind comes to him. Meditation is abruptly brought to a halt. This is another variety of the unconscious protective reaction. Like the jerking of the body, the panic reaction ceases with a little practise of meditation.

This reaction occurred in a businessman some six weeks ago. He had been tense for as long as he could remember and was getting little or no help from the tranquillisers which he had been taking for years. During his second session he became quite white and started to sweat profusely. Afterwards, he told me of an acute feeling of panic. At the next session he had a very slight transient panic reaction, and subsequently no panics at all. His longstanding anxiety has been reduced and he now speaks of himself literally as a new man.

Our anxiety is greatly reduced by the presence of a trusted teacher. We unconsciously feel they are there, they know, they understand, they will look after us, they will see that nothing goes wrong. These ideas do not come to our full consciousness. But they are there. We have a greater feeling of security. Our anxiety is reduced, and it is so much the easier to let ourself be. The presence of the teacher helps. But we can in fact learn to let ourself be, just by ourselves, without the presence of any teacher at all. My evidence for stating this so dogmatically is in some hundreds of letters that I have received from people all over the world telling me of their improved health and state of mind after practising the simple mental exercises described in my book *Relief Without Drugs*.

At first we may be prevented from letting ourselves fully participate by unconscious psychological protective reactions. This may seem strange to the reader. You may say, 'Surely we can let ourselves do what we want to do.' But, of course, very often we can't. Reactions at one level of our mind prevent us doing things that we wish to do at another level. Thus our conscience prevents us doing things that, at a lower level of our mind, we would like to do. In the present instance the opposite situation prevails. The upper, voluntary level of our mind is prevented from doing what it wishes by the lower, more primitive, protective level. Over countless generations we have learned the importance of being on guard. This has become bred into us as those who were not on guard did not survive to have progeny. This is something that we cannot easily put aside. Letting ourself go. This is unguarded behaviour. It is risky. Inborn protective mechanisms hold us back. We find that we cannot let go really freely, although we would very much like to do so.

We can get around the unconscious protective reactions that prevent us from letting go. We do this by repetition. Familiarity brings a sense of security. Each time we relax, it is as though our unconscious mind lets us go a little further. Gradually it learns that no harm comes to us from this experience, we find that we are no longer holding ourselves back, and we are able to let go more freely.

Those of us who are tense and anxious have more difficulty in letting go in Mental Ataraxis than do those who are more secure. This is what we would expect. Anxiety alerts all our defensive reactions. So those with a high level of anxiety have more difficulty in the initial stages of Mental Ataraxis. But if you are tense, don't be discouraged. There is a kind of paradox in this. The tense person, who usually has greater initial difficulties, also gets greater initial benefit as the relief of his tension is immediately felt as a significant move towards a better life.

The most common barrier to the relaxation of the mind is the persistence of unwanted thoughts. We can't stop thinking. We can't turn off our thoughts. Our mind goes on and on churning things over. Sometimes it is everyday affairs, what we must do at the office, what we will cook for dinner tonight, when will we see our girlfriend again, what should we do for the children? It is clear that such thoughts prevent the relaxation of mind which we are seeking. We try to relax, to put the thoughts out of our mind, but the more we try, the more persistent are the thoughts. We become frustrated and angry with ourselves that we cannot do this simple thing.

There are two distinct types of unwanted thoughts. One type concerns the realistic thoughts pertaining to everyday problems. These thoughts are reasoned. They are logical and sensible. The other type of thought occurs when our mind runs free. It flits about, jumping from subject to subject, wandering here and there without any clear connection between one subject and the next. We only become aware that our mental relaxation has been interrupted by our thoughts when our thinking stops for a moment. We then realise that we have been working out some practical problem or alternatively that our mind has been running wild, just flitting about from subject to subject.

We must avoid getting angry with ourselves because we cannot stop the unwanted thoughts. We must remember that this is a very common difficulty and in the early stages most people have at least some trouble in this respect. Even eastern mystics, both Yogis and Zen practitioners, have admitted to me that they have this trouble. But the person learning Mental Ataraxis can be reassured by the fact that with most people this difficulty settles down with a little practice. The important point is that these unwanted thoughts should not disturb us.

Unwanted thoughts that are realistic can be quietened simply by feeling the relaxation of our body. When things are going well we do not feel the relaxation of our limbs. We are merely participating in the total experience of relaxation. But we can do so temporarily in order to quieten these thoughts. We feel the relaxation of our arms as they rest on the sides of the chair. They are so relaxed we just feel the weight of them. The relaxed heaviness.

And the same with our legs. Relaxed. And the feeling of the weight of them on the floor. And our face. We feel the relaxation of our face muscles. In this way we keep our mind occupied on feeling the relaxation. As long as it is occupied with feeling, the thoughts cease.

This is very effective in stopping our unwanted thoughts, and in this it is a step in the right direction. We soon find that our mind requires less and less direction to the feeling of relaxation, and the unwanted thoughts themselves become less and less insistent. We are able gradually to change from the conscious feeling of relaxation to the simpler mental process of just experiencing it, and the relaxation of our mind is able to continue without the intrusion of unwanted thoughts.

When our unwanted thoughts are merely flitting about in unreasoned fashion we can simply let them run on and our essential mental relaxation remains undisturbed. This is possible because of the uncontrolled nature of these thoughts. It is rather similar to what happens in a day-dream or reverie. We can just let them run on, and they gradually settle down. The important point is not to be cross with ourselves when we suddenly realise that we have been subject to this type of mental activity when we were hoping for real quietness of our mind.

Once we have learned to relax our mind in this way we no longer need to concern ourselves about experiencing the relaxation of our body. All that we have been discussing is merely a teaching programme for our mind, as it were. Once our mind has learned how to do it, there is no need for us to repeat these preliminary steps each time. We now know what we want, and our mind has learned how to attain it. When we want to relax our mind, the relaxation of it is just there, quite naturally, in the stillness and the completeness of it all.

Body relaxed; mind relaxed; more than our body and our mind; it is our whole being. We experience the completeness of the relaxation. It is in every aspect of ourself. The ease of our muscles pervades our thought and feeling. Conscious only of ease. Arms, legs, trunk, shoulders are only ease. The stillness of our thought is ease. So is the calm of our mind and all feeling gives way to ease.

The fact that the relaxation is not simply of our body, and not simply of our mind, but is of our whole being brings a sense of integration and unity. There are no separate parts. A profound unity. Something deep. We sense this unity as our inner being.

Oneness, our indivisible self. In this way we far transcend simple mechanistic approaches in which the subject is encouraged to feel the relaxation in different muscles or different parts of his body.

Just let me warn you of one thing in particular. Please do not get the feeling that Mental Ataraxis is something complicated. It isn't. It is a matter of extreme simplicity. It is only the words that we have to use to describe it that make it seem complicated. I have just read over the foregoing chapter, and I am prompted to issue this warning. Please accept what I say about this. The experience of Mental Ataraxis is a matter of very great simplicity, but the description of it is necessarily complicated. This is so with many events in our ordinary life. To stand up is a simple matter for all of us. But to describe the anatomical, physiological and neurological processes involved in standing up may well fill a very complex text. But the experience remains simple; so it is with Mental Ataraxis, except that it only comes to us with some degree of guidance.

5

OUR POSTURE FOR MENTAL ATARAXIS

Sitting in our armchair we have learned to let our body relax physically, we have learned to experience this relaxation as part of our whole self, and in this way we have brought it into our mind. The next step in Mental Ataraxis is to let our mind experience this relaxation while we are in less comfortable postures.

There are many reasons why we should assume a definite posture to practise our Mental Ataraxis. We have started our venture sitting in an armchair, but you will remember that I warned against letting ourselves just slump in the chair, and I emphasised the importance of maintaining a symmetrical position without allowing our head to fall forward. So we are already familiar with the rudiments of posture, and now the time has come to move out of our armchair and practise our Mental Ataraxis in circumstances that are slightly more demanding of us.

A definite posture is necessary for Mental Ataraxis in order to provide circumstances of initial slight discomfort. This is something of the greatest importance. We shall discuss the matter in some detail in the next chapter. For the present let us accept the idea that in Mental Ataraxis we need to commence our meditation in circumstances of slight discomfort. Then, as our meditation proceeds, we cease to be aware of our initial slight discomfort. This transcendence of slight discomfort is an essential feature of Mental Ataraxis, and it is conveniently arranged by assuming a posture suitable to our own individual personal needs.

By assuming a definite posture we ensure that the relaxation of our mind comes about through the mind itself and not from the physical comfort of our body. This is an important point. If we just flop on our bed, warm and comfortable, we achieve some relaxation of our mind. In these circumstances the relaxed state of our mind is brought about by the nerve endings in our arms and legs and body reporting to our brain via the sensory nerves that all is well and comfortable. The level of neurological excitation of our brain is reduced and we experience it as the feeling of being relaxed in our mind.

This situation gives us rest, and within the very limited scope of rest, we are benefited. But this type of mental relaxation has no lasting effect at all on our general level of nervous tension, our various psychosomatic disorders and discomforts, or our experience of life in general.

The same applies to the mental relaxation which comes to us when flopped comfortably in an armchair, or lying sprawled on the beach in warm sunshine. Hence the importance of our posture in Mental Ataraxis which ensures that the relaxation of our mind comes from the mind itself and is not simply induced in superficial fashion by bodily comfort.

By assuming a definite posture for our Mental Ataraxis we establish the idea of easy control and self discipline. This of course is what we are aiming to achieve. Easy control and self discipline. We are now starting on the path of the *Discipline of Ease* which is the way of life which comes to us through Mental Ataraxis. In one sense the maintenance of a definite posture is a task which involves some effort and some difficulty. But in Mental Ataraxis, with the relaxation of our mind, the same task becomes quite effortless and involves no difficulty whatsoever. In this way our meditating in a definite posture becomes a learning experience of the highest importance leading our mind in a practical way into the Discipline of Ease.

By assuming a definite posture we prevent ourselves falling asleep. This is a practical matter. Only last week a middle aged businessman, who had been extremely tense prior to practising Mental Ataraxis, complained of going to sleep while meditating. This is quite a common problem. The interesting aspect about the businessman of last week is the way in which a man, who only a few weeks ago was so tense, edgy, irritable, restless and generally over-alert, could so quickly let himself go to sleep. If you should experience this trouble yourself, the solution is simple and it never fails. You simply use a slightly more uncomfortable posture.

In Mental Ataraxis it does not matter what posture we assume provided certain conditions are satisfied. Our posture must provide some initial slight discomfort which we transcend as our meditation proceeds, so that our relaxation comes from the mind itself and not from the comfort of our body. It must give us the feeling of doing with ease something which is really slightly difficult, and it must be such that it prevents us falling asleep. Beyond these considerations the actual nature of our physical posture is immaterial.

Mental Ataraxis veers away from most other approaches, traditional and modern, in that the only demand made upon posture is that the position adopted ensures discomfort so that the relaxation comes from the mind and not the body. Some eastern schools advocate the use of special postures for special purposes. Thus different postures are used in attempts to relieve disorder in different organs of the body. We can, in fact, influence the function of different organs through meditation. Our heart rate is a simple example. But the effect on our organs comes about through action of our mind and not directly by any effect on the organ itself through some specific posture.

Mental relaxation in the absence of a definite posture may bring us rest, but it reduces our capacity for self-discipline. Let us look at it this way. We need rest, both of our body and our mind. It gives us ease. On the other hand, relaxation of our mind, and the rest that it brings, can become a kind of hedonistic pastime in itself – a way to material nothingness, and mental and spiritual emptiness. We want more than this, although not harsh self-discipline; nor do we want something puritanical nor masochistic. We are striving for something better – the Discipline of Ease.

From both my patients and my fellows I have learned that it eludes those who are given to enjoy, too much, the mental relaxation of rest. To overcome this we should be flexible in our choice of posture for Mental Ataraxis. We want to avoid meditating in one particular posture simply as a matter of habit. By being flexible we keep our mind open for new experiences.

By changing about and meditating one time in one posture and another time in some other posture we facilitate the transition of the effects of our meditation into our daily life. For many eastern mystics meditation is an end in itself. This is not so with us. As we see it, it is life itself that counts, its quality and its fullness. Our Mental Ataraxis is a means towards this end. We seek to enjoy the ease of mind which we experience in meditation in our ordinary life while we are actively doing things. If we always meditate in the same posture, we come to associate the ease of meditation with these particular circumstances. This is not what we want. By changing about in the circumstances of our meditation we develop the idea that the ease of our mind is with us, whatever we are doing. As this comes to us we are moving towards the Discipline of Ease in our daily life.

It is easy to make the transition from meditation in our armchair to meditating in an upright chair. It is both easy and necessary. It is easy because we have accustomed ourselves to the idea that meditation is a mental process and is not dependent on our being comfortable. When we come to do it, we sit in the upright chair so that we ourselves are upright, and during the whole of our meditation we maintain our upright position without slumping forward. When I meditate in an upright chair I like to start by visualising a statue of the seated Pharaoh. So upright, so calm, and such ease about it all. By the process of identification I come to feel myself in this posture. Arms are on my thighs. Just resting there. They are so relaxed I feel the natural weight of them on my thighs and I am aware of the utter relaxation of my biceps muscles. Head is erect. It is erect yet at the same time easy. Then it comes to me more completely. The statue of the Pharaoh fades. I am no longer aware of my relaxation. Only calm. Deeper and deeper.

The transition from our armchair to the upright chair is a necessary step in our Mental Ataraxis. We can go so far in our armchair, then the time comes and we must make a move to go further. Sometimes when I have asked patients how they have been getting on, they have disclosed that they have not made the move from the armchair. They have usually explained that they seemed to be doing quite well in the armchair so could see no need for any change. Quite incredible! But we are all liable to become content with our own mediocrity. It is like the people who say, 'I am not very tense, why should I worry about meditation.' My patients had got stuck in their armchair from their own inertia and their failure to strive for something better, so that they were incapable of that minimal effort to move to another chair.

I repeat that the move *is* necessary. Then, when we have done it a few times, like the Egyptian Pharaoh, we can make another slight advance. We do it sitting on the edge of the chair so that our back is no longer in contact with the back of the chair. We can then make a further transition to sitting on a stool. We can now change from having our legs straight with our feet flat on the floor, as in the Pharaoh posture, to having our legs crossed. This makes it so much the easier for us to change to meditating in a squatting posture.

In the upright chair we are much more aware of our need to maintain our posture and much more aware that our mental relaxation is, in fact, due to an act of our mind. We are aware of these matters as we start, but as our Mental Ataraxis comes to us this awareness fades into our general experience of calm. During the first few sessions we may find that our head slowly sags forward, and we have to bring it back to the upright position. We soon find that when this happens we are so relaxed in our mind that moving our head back does not disturb the experience of calm which has come about us. With a little practice we find that our head is maintained in the upright position without conscious effort on our part. It just stays there. Quite effortlessly. And our mind is learning something of the Discipline of Ease.

We can meditate lying on the floor. We can do it on the floor, but never in bed. Bed is too comfortable, and the experience of ease comes from nerve endings in our body and not by act of our mind. We just lie flat on our back. Hands by our sides. We may need something under the head just at first until we become accustomed to it. A book is sufficient to raise the head a little. Cushions or pillows are best avoided as making us too comfortable. Some elderly patients have told me that they place a cushion under the legs behind the knees. This may be a reasonable compromise for older people with stiff joints.

The move to lying on the floor is a help to those who have had difficulty in obtaining really complete muscular relaxation in the armchair. As we become familiar with the idea of doing it lying on the floor, we can add to this experience by placing small objects under our back between the shoulderblades. This adds to our initial feeling of being slightly uncomfortable. A few pebbles serve the purpose quite well, so do children's toy blocks or small metallic toys, or even an ashtray. As we lie on these things, the discomfort at first is quite marked. Then we let ourselves go, the discomfort eases, and soon we are quite unaware of it.

For the first time we do it, the most difficult phase is when we first experience the full weight of our body on the object. For a moment the discomfort may be quite intense. At this moment, we feel the relaxation in our face. Relaxed. Face utterly relaxed. Feeling it. Deeply in our face. The discomfort in our back has eased. We relax all over. Letting ourself go with it. Letting our body melt into the thing on our back. The discomfort has all gone. Only calm. Deep calm, all through us.

Squatting with legs crossed is the most generally satisfactory posture for those who can manage it. We squat on the floor, our legs crossed in front of us. Our back straight and our head held erect. Remember that we are seeking a posture that is slightly uncomfortable, but the discomfort must not be so great that we cannot transcend it so that the discomfort gives way to the general experience of ease. Bearing this in mind, most of us need a little help in the squatting posture. This comes if we sit on something to raise our buttocks an inch or even two inches above the level of the floor. So squat on a cushion or a pillow or better still, on a telephone book. This takes some of the strain off our joints, and we are better able to maintain our back in a perpendicular position.

It is easier to squat on a hard unyielding surface, such as the floor, rather than on something soft such as our bed or a couch or a mattress. When we squat on a hard surface, our buttocks and our heels remain at the same level. But owing to the weight of our body, our buttocks sink into a soft surface so that our heels are higher than our buttocks which places greater strain on the ligaments of our hip joints.

It is quite important that we should have our back as upright as possible. The reason for this is that it requires less muscular effort to maintain ourselves in a well balanced position than if we let ourselves lean forward. When we are well-balanced, and we have transcended the initial discomfort, we can maintain ourselves in this position quite effortlessly and the calm of our Mental Ataraxis is not interrupted by any conscious straining to maintain the posture. I myself, when I first squat down, like to feel my body straighten by stretching upwards. The feeling of stretching upwards seems to give me the easy balance that we need. Sitting upwards. Upwardness. Then as the meditation experience comes, the feeling of stretching upwards fades.

In the squatting posture, the complete relaxation of the muscles of our legs increases the discomfort from the tension in the ligaments, then the discomfort fades as we relax our mind. This involves a natural protective reflex. The muscles automatically contract so as to take the strain off the joints, thus saving us from discomfort and pain. This is a simple protective reaction. But this is not what we are seeking. We are aiming to transcend the discomfort by act of mind which is something quite different.

If, when we first squat down, we are a little stiff in the joints, it is likely that our knees do not rest on the floor, but remain held up in the air. If we now use our hand to feel the muscles of our thighs, and especially the muscles in the groin, we will feel that they are quite tense. The tension in the muscles is taking some of the weight of our legs and so relieving strain on the ligaments. This defeats our purpose. We must let the muscles relax and experience this slight discomfort so that we can then transcend it by our own ease of mind.

Bringing our leg muscles to let go takes practice. We often think that they are relaxed when, in fact, they have not let go at all. We can test this very easily by letting our hand rest in our groin where we feel the iliacus muscle which extends from the crest of the pelvis to the top of the hip bone. When the muscle relaxes we can feel it quite easily with our hand. In my own case, I have often felt it relax quite satisfactorily, but then, when I have felt it a few moments later, it has been quite tense again. We must expect fluctuations like this. For a while our muscles relax very completely and our knees are let down so that they touch, or almost touch, the floor. But a few moments later we notice that our knees have risen up again as a result of recurring tension in the muscles. We let them go again, but there is a tendency for these fluctuations in tension to recur until we have mastered the relaxation fairly completely.

In the squatting posture, the relaxation of our arms is easy because there is no undue tension on the arm joints. We can just let our arms hang loosely by our side with our hands resting on the floor. I have noticed that the relaxation seems more complete if the outside of the hand is in contact with the floor rather than the palm. If we choose we can let our hands rest on our knees. This adds to the ease of our position by giving greater stability. Also in this position it is very easy to feel the relaxation of the biceps muscles and the natural weight of our arm on our knee. This has an additional effect in that the weight of our arms on our knees helps to keep our knees down and relax the muscles of the thighs.

Alternatively we can let our hands rest in our groins or we can hold them in front of us with our fingers interlocking if we so wish.

Most people can, in fact, manage the squatting posture without too much effort or discomfort. Just remember that all we are aiming to do is to find a position of slight discomfort in which to meditate. The fruits of the meditative process are then within our reach, within our grasp, and that is what really counts.

The squatting posture provides opportunity for the complete relaxation of some muscle groups and at the same time the maintenance of tone in others, and so enhances our experience of simultaneous relaxation and control. Controlled ease. The Discipline of Ease. This is what we are seeking.

As we proceed with our Mental Ataraxis in the squatting posture, our arms are completely relaxed. Free. There is nothing holding back this relaxation. Our legs are also relaxed, and if we are doing it well their relaxation is complete, but this has been more difficult because the relaxation of our legs tends to cause discomfort from tension in the ligaments. But our back and neck muscles are not completely relaxed. If they were we would fall over. But the ease of our mind is such that the tension in our back and neck is quite effortless and does not intrude into our awareness.

Beyond this there is another group of muscles which can add further to our experiences of simultaneous ease and control. These are the abdominal muscles, particularly the muscles of the lower abdomen. When I first squat down, I relax very completely, and as I do so I notice that the lower part of my tummy protrudes despite the fact that I am thin by nature. This protrusion of the lower part of the abdomen is natural enough because my general relaxation has relaxed the tone of the muscles which normally hold in my tummy. So, as I proceed with my Mental Ataraxis, I consciously bring these muscles to contract. I do this very easily and naturally so that the tone remains in these muscles without any further conscious effort on my part. Just like the muscles of my back and neck, the tummy muscles remain doing what they ought to do quite effortlessly and my mind learns from this simultaneous experience of complete relaxation and effortless control.

There is a more complete version of the squatting posture sometimes known as the perfect posture in which the knees rest firmly on the floor and the foot of one leg rests on the ankle of the other leg. This is half way, as it were, towards the lotus posture. Many eastern teachers of both Yoga and Zen hold that the ability to sit in this position is a necessary prerequisite before commencing meditation. We have already discussed the fact that in Mental Ataraxis a set position is not necessary. Nevertheless, this is a very satisfactory posture for meditation on account of its greater physical stability over the more loosely contrived squatting posture which we have just discussed. Most people who practise in the squatting posture sense this, and do in fact try to bring their knees down to rest firmly on the floor and thus move towards the perfect posture.

We can meditate in a kneeling posture. We kneel as if in prayer, but our arms hang loosely by our side, and our head is inclined slightly forward. This posture has two significant attributes. In the first place kneeling is the posture for Christian prayer. There is a symbolic significance about it. So meditation in a kneeling posture brings us to associate our meditation with religious experience. I know from talking with patients that many people do in fact come to regard their Mental Ataraxis as something religious. From my experiences it would seem that this is most common, not in those who are religious in the orthodox church-going fashion, but in sensitive people who have an active inner spiritual life of their own. Meditation easily becomes a part of this inner spiritual experience. If you, the reader, happen to be either a rather extravert person or religious in the orthodox sense, it is likely that this idea of an association between your meditation and religion will never have occurred to you. But a surprising number of people have talked along these lines to me. They have often been people who feel the seasons and natural rhythm of things as a manifestation of some divine power. The stillness, the ease and the naturalness of meditation seems to be part of it. And they find that the experience is enhanced by sometimes meditating in a kneeling posture.

In the kneeling posture we need to maintain much greater control. This is obvious. In kneeling we have to maintain tone in many more muscles to prevent ourselves falling over than we do when sitting or squatting. This works for the development of easy control in real life situations, and in this way becomes a further step towards the Discipline of Ease.

We can meditate kneeling with our buttocks resting on our heels. This is another way of kneeling. Fat people with large thighs may find it difficult or impossible. If this be the case the difficulty is easily overcome by kneeling in the upright position and placing a cushion over your heels and then sitting back so that your buttocks come to rest on the cushion. In this way your knees are not bent so acutely and the position is so much the easier to maintain.

We can also meditate kneeling in an upright position with our knees well apart. Our arms hang by our side, and unlike the prayer posture our head is held erect. This posture gives us the same need for control as the prayer posture without the overlay of religious feeling.

There are possible minor dangers associated with some postures.
I have never met anyone who has suffered ill effects as a result
of these dangers. Nevertheless I feel that I should draw your
attention to them.

There is possible danger in prolonged meditation with the eyes open.
With most people the eyes close spontaneously as meditation
commences. There are however a few people who maintain a
fixed unblinking stare. I always advise such people to close their
eyes. There are some sects of Zen Buddhism who practise zazen
meditation with their eyes open. As I see it, the possible dangers
are threefold. There is the obvious danger of being struck in the
eye by a flying insect. There is also the danger that the surface
of the transparent membrane in front of the pupil, the cornea,
could become dry and eroded through absence of blinking. In
ordinary circumstances the continual blinking of our eyelids
keeps the outer surface of the cornea moist. The third possible
danger arises with the eyes open in bright light, if the gaze should
be fixed in the general direction of the sun, the absence of
movement of the eyeball could possibly lead to the focusing of
light and heat on one small area of the retina with consequent
danger to the sensitive retinal cells. Perhaps I am more conscious
than others of these potential dangers as they are greater when
meditating out of doors which is what I myself prefer.

*When meditating sitting in a chair with wooden arms there is danger
from pressure on the radial nerve if the arm should be allowed to
hang downwards over the arm of the chair.* In my student days
this condition was known as 'drunk' paralysis' as it occasionally
happened when a drunk was 'sleeping it off' in a chair with his
arm hanging in this position. Over the last few years I have been
showing people how to experience Mental Ataraxis in public
groups of fifty or sixty. The room which I have for this purpose
is furnished with chairs with wooden arms. It is quite common
during the session for the arm of a meditator to slip off and hang
down in the danger position over the wooden arm of the chair.
When this happens I simply pick up the arm and restore it either
to the arm of the chair, or let it rest safely on the person's thigh.

*For men there is a possible danger in prolonged meditation in the
squatting posture with the heel under the perineum.* The danger is
that the tube which bears urine from the bladder to the penis,
the urethra, could be bruised by pressure from the pubic bone

above pressing down on the heel of the foot. This potential danger is easily averted by keeping the heel further forward so that the urethra cannot be squashed between it and the pubic bone.

There is danger of a stiff neck if we allow our head to fall forwards on to our chest. This is obvious enough. The very complete relaxation of the muscles leaves the ligaments unsupported by the normal tone of the muscles around the joints, and they take the full strain of supporting the weight of the head. Sometimes the head of one of the meditators in my group falls forward in this fashion. When this happens I slowly move the head back to the upright position, hold it there for a moment, and then release it. On almost all occasions the head has then remained in the correct upright position of its own accord. An interesting point is that my moving the head does not appear to interrupt the profound relaxation of the meditator. In fact, when I have spoken to some of them afterwards it has seemed that they had scant recollection of the incident.

When should we meditate? There are a couple of guiding principles. In the first place, if we are using our Mental Ataraxis to get help from asthma or migraine or other periodic psychosomatic conditions, we get much greater help by practising when we are free of symptoms rather than waiting for the symptoms to develop and then trying to relieve them. By practising when we are free of symptoms we are less likely to have an attack, as we then do not over-react to stress in the same way and so precipitate an attack. I have had many patients with both asthma and migraine who have learned how to stop an attack by Mental Ataraxis as soon as they feel it coming on. But the best time to practise is between the attacks, when we are feeling well.

We get much more out of our meditation, irrespective of the purpose for which we are doing it, if we practise when we are not too tired. People have often said to me that they had thought that a certain degree of fatigue would help their relaxation. This is not so. They have been making the mistake of thinking of relaxation in terms of bodily comfort and the drowsiness of fatigue rather than as an act of mind. Not long ago a successful middle-aged businessman told me he had read my book *Relief Without Drugs* and had been practising the mental exercises I describe in it. He went on to tell me that each day when he came home from his office, he would sit down by the fire. (The incident happened in winter.) He would have a couple of whiskies and read the evening paper for half an hour. Then he would do his mental exercises for fifteen minutes. Hopeless! Yet he thought he had caught on to what I am trying to teach!

Immediately after our bath or shower is a very good time to meditate. People say, 'But I am in such a terrible rush in the mornings.' I say, 'If you will just capture it for two or three minutes, you will do things more easily and then you will not be in such a terrible rush.' We all get into the way of doing things by routine and habit. In a way this is good as it saves us the mental energy of having to make decisions over trivial matters.

What I ask you to do is this. Just add another small item to the habitual routine. Now, before you dress for the day – perhaps immediately after your bath or shower – squat for just two or three minutes, just long enough to capture the experience of mental relaxation. Now get dressed, and off you go. These two or three minutes may save you a great deal of time through your greater efficiency and ease during the morning.

We want to develop the attitude of mind in which we look forward to and enjoy our periods of practice. This is not difficult as the feeling of calm and ease which comes to us is extremely enjoyable. But at the start everyone is not fully aware of this because they have not experienced it. And I know of some people who have approached their practice in an unappreciative attitude of mind as if they were forcing themselves to perform some unpleasant duty or chore. As a result of this, their anxiety is increased, their attention alerted and the whole process is negated.

If you are practising primarily for the relief of psychosomatic symptoms, do not discontinue practice immediately the symptoms are relieved. This would seem obvious enough, yet I have encountered a number of people who have fallen into this trap. Their symptoms have been relieved. They ceased to practise. The level of their anxiety has risen again, and the symptoms have returned. The permanent relief of psychosomatic disorders necessitates the reduction of anxiety. This is not too difficult. But it requires two things. The continuation of the exercises for some time after the symptoms have gone, and bringing the mental relaxation which is attained during practice into our ordinary day to day life. By this means there comes about a permanent reduction of anxiety.

Where should we meditate? Again, there are some guiding principles. At the start we do not want to make things too difficult
for ourselves; accordingly it is sensible to commence our venture
into Mental Ataraxis in reasonably quiet surroundings so that
we are not distracted by extraneous noise. But I have tried to
give you the feeling that Mental Ataraxis is a progressive experience. So it is in this. And we progress from doing it in quiet
surroundings to situations of normal noise and distraction. This
is important.

We must avoid conditioning ourselves so that we can only
experience Mental Ataraxis in circumstances of peace and quiet.
If we were to do this we would not be able to bring the effects
of it so readily into our everyday life. So we start in quiet
surroundings, and as soon as we begin to capture it, we practise
when deliberately exposing ourselves to all the usual noises of
everyday life.

I remember, some time ago, asking a woman patient how she
was getting on with the practice of Mental Ataraxis. She explained to me that she had not been able to practise because
there was usually someone else in the house! If we can capture
mental relaxation only in ideal conditions we are not making
much progress on the way to ease of mind.

On the other hand, to give you an example of the other extreme I have several patients who practise very effectively on the
crowded train each morning as they commute into the city. I
know of two busy housewives who can capture it very completely
while sitting in the family circle looking at TV. They sit rather
at the back, and while the others are preoccupied with the
programme, they let their eyes close, and as the Mental Ataraxis
comes to them the TV. voices become blurred and meaningless
and finally fade from consciousness.

I personally enjoy Mental Ataraxis outside in the open air. To me,
the air, the wind, the sunshine, the rustle of the leaves, the song
of the birds, all add to the experience. Let us look upon Mental
Ataraxis as an experience of life in the aspect of all its natural
ease and harmony. If the wind is fierce and the cold chilling we
still maintain the experience of ease and the feeling of the natural
harmony remains with us. As our Mental Ataraxis becomes more
complete, our awareness of all this becomes less vivid until it
finally fades. But it is still there, somehow influencing us even
though it is not through our clear consciousness. To me this is
a much more satisfying approach than that of the monk quietly
meditating in his cell or the Yogi in some mountain cave, or

Daruma the Zen mystic who meditated for seven years with his face to the wall.

What do we wear to meditate? The answer is simple. We wear as little as we can without offending those about us, and sufficient to prevent us becoming chilled. There is great power in symbolism. Clothes that allow us freedom reflect a sense of freedom within. When we meditate after our shower, of course we do so naked. Where I once lived I had a swimming pool at the bottom of the garden which was not overlooked by either the neighbours or the house. I enjoyed meditating squatting naked by the pool after my swim. I used to do this, both in the blistering heat of the summer and in the chill winds of winter, and I am sure I gained a lot by it. There are several aspects to Mental Ataraxis. One aspect is the experience of life in its true simplicity. Nakedness helps us towards it.

For how long should we meditate? It depends on the individual. I once spent some time with a very saintly old Yogi in the Himalayas near Katmandu. He meditated for sixteen hours every day. He had two hours sleep and six hours of ordinary wakefulness. This was his life.

However, this is not for us. We want to experience the reality of this life we live, the love and the compassion, the challenge and the striving. We want to participate in these things to the full. To live life. But we aim to live it with ease and naturalness. Even to meet the challenge and the striving with ease and naturalness. This is what the Discipline of Ease is all about. I learned a great deal from the saintly old Yogi in the Himalayas, and I openly acknowledge my debt to him. But we are seeking different things. To him meditation was an end in itself, to us it is the means to a better life. If we were to follow his example we would not have time for the reality of living.

Most of us can make very great changes for the better with ten minutes Mental Ataraxis two or three times a day. This short period is effective because the thing which really counts is the way in which we let the effects of our Mental Ataraxis come into our daily life.

Strangely enough, only this morning I saw a very tense young man, a clerk of courts by occupation, who is at the same time studying for a degree in law. He told me when I last saw him that he had been practising Mental Ataraxis between three and four hours each day. I told him that I thought that this was too long. I subsequently discovered that he had become preoccupied about the subjective experience of Mental Ataraxis. He kept striving for a greater and greater feeling of it. He was judging his success by what he felt during his meditation and not by the effect of his meditation on his experience of life. He had lost the ease and effortlessness of it; he found himself striving for something which kept receding like a mirage, and so he forced himself to prolong the experience more and more.

6

MEDITATING IN DISCOMFORT

We have now learned to meditate in various postures. Our next step in Mental Ataraxis is to learn to transcend discomfort through relaxation of our mind.

I have overwhelming evidence for the importance of discomfort in meditation. It rests on my experience with many hundreds of patients. There is no doubt whatsoever that those patients who have combined the judicious use of discomfort with their meditative practice have, in fact, gained much more from the experience. I could quote you many case histories to prove the point. The common situation has been that the person has read my book *Relief Without Drugs* and has practised the mental exercises I described. But they have practised only in half-hearted fashion, disregarding my advice about the use of discomfort.

Even with this incomplete venture into Mental Ataraxis most of these people have had some help, but most of them feel that they could gain more. This is what has brought them to see me. I particularly recall one doctor, a surgeon. I remember well his opening words, 'I have read all about your relaxing and it does not work.' When I asked more about it, he disclosed that he had been practising lying on his bed. His explanation was, 'Because you are more relaxed that way.' As soon as I got him doing it properly, his symptoms disappeared, and he finally became quite a convert. Interestingly enough, he has become a much less aggressive person and very much easier to get along with, not only with me but also with his family and staff.

As we relax, our mind transcends the discomfort of our posture and then there is no discomfort. This is really the most important aspect of the whole process of meditation. It is the getting beyond discomfort which allows us to experience the essential stillness of mind. In this way it is not the transcendence of discomfort in itself which we seek, but rather the state of mind which goes with it.

The transcendence of minor discomfort in Mental Ataraxis deepens the meditative process. Although there are objective methods of determining the depth of meditation by means of electro-encephalography, we can, in fact, estimate the depth which we have attained by the subjective phenomena which we have experienced. Please note that I write this in the past tense. It is only afterwards that we realise that we have been deep. Any awareness of our state of mind at the time of meditation means that we are not deep as we are obviously functioning at a critical level. But afterwards we can be aware that we have been oblivious of our surroundings and experiencing stillness of mind. This depth of meditation comes to us more easily and more completely when we have transcended some degree of discomfort.

Both Christian mystics and the mystics of the east have long realised the importance of the transcendence of discomfort. The monk's cell and personal flagellation have been the means by which Christians have achieved this end, whereas in the East it is attained through the discomfort of the meditative posture. There is a common belief among Europeans that the cross-legged squatting posture is comfortable for Asiatic peoples. This is true in the general sense when the legs are crossed loosely without much strain on the ligaments of the joints. But from my experience in the East I have learned that the meditating Yogi or Zen practitioner is always striving to keep his legs in tighter and tighter posture, so that his position for meditation is always one of potential discomfort.

At first the degree of discomfort should be very small indeed. Just enough to be very slightly uncomfortable. By starting with only a minimum of discomfort we do not set ourselves a task that is beyond our ability to achieve. This slight degree of discomfort can be attained simply by sitting on the edge of a **straight-backed** chair without resting against the back of it. To sit on a stool is quite effective, or to squat loosely on the floor without putting too much strain on the ligaments, or simply to lie flat on one's back on the floor.

In transcending minor discomfort in Mental Ataraxis we reduce the level of our anxiety. Our mind has the ability to reduce anxiety and restore calm and ease provided suitable circumstances are provided for this mechanism to operate. The depth of meditation which we achieve in getting beyond discomfort provides the circumstances in which this natural ability of our mind can function effectively. The reduction of anxiety has the effect of relieving psychosomatic symptoms and the development of openness of our personality through the absence of defensive attitudes.

If we make ourselves so uncomfortable that we are unable to transcend the discomfort, the whole process fails, and the level of our anxiety is increased. So do not rush into this aspect of Mental Ataraxis too quickly. Just take it little by little. Let the conditioning process work slowly, naturally, easily. And then there is no danger of a temporary setback by being confronted with a degree of discomfort which is beyond our capacity to handle.

By learning to transcend discomfort in meditation we are better able to manage physical discomfort in other areas of our life. Discomfort no longer worries us to the same extent. If need be, we can sit relaxed on an uncomfortable seat, as our mind has learned to ignore such things.

By learning to transcend physical discomfort in meditation we are better able to manage mental discomfort in real life. We are able to get beyond the mental hurt of things. As civilisation advances we are spared more and more the physical discomforts of the body, but at the same time we are becoming more vulnerable to hurts of the mind. The sadness from loss of friendship, the hurt of some trivial slight or humiliation, these are the matters which now concern us more than the discomforts of the body. By bringing ourselves to transcend physical discomfort in meditation we learn to cope better with these matters of the mind. The very simple self discipline of learning to transcend discomfort in meditation helps us to establish an easy self discipline for life itself.

I would stress the two points. In meditation it is very easy to acquire the self discipline of transcending physical discomfort. Secondly, an easy, natural type of self discipline is an essential part of successful living. The one follows the other very easily and very naturally. The simple self discipline of meditation leads us to the greater and equally simple self discipline in the practical affairs of life.

Some people are inclined to baulk at the idea of imposing any discomfort on themselves, however slight it might be. We have within us a primitive psychological mechanism which leads us to experience pleasure and to avoid pain or discomfort. This is of obvious value to us. To voluntarily impose discomfort on ourselves runs contrary to this biological principle. So we tend to shy away from such an idea. However this is a very primitive reaction. The fact is that we learn to accept many discomforts of the present in order to gain things in the future.

Man learned this when he first laboured tilling the soil in the expectation of the reward of the harvest. The present-day student endures the hardship of study for better things to come. So do we all as we save for the future. In this perspective the management of the self-inflicted discomfort of Mental Ataraxis is seen as a very natural move in our progression to a better life.

In the wilful experience of discomfort we must clearly distinguish between the high purpose of training our mind and the perversion of simple masochism. We must remember that masochism is a personality trait which has been, and still is, biologically useful to us. We can see its origin in very primitive times.

When sex was an act dictated purely by physiological need, the male often forced himself upon the female. In these circumstances, the woman who could mingle pleasure with the hurt of sexual experience would have more frequent intercourse and greater progeny, so that the trait of masochism has become bred into us, more so in women than men. On the other hand, we have evolved another psychological reaction which, like masochism, has led us wilfully to tolerate discomfort. This is the process by which we have learned to deny ourselves the pleasure of the moment in the expectation of better or greater pleasure in the future. It is to this latter reaction that the experience of discomfort in Mental Ataraxis belongs.

7

MENTAL ATARAXIS IN EVERYDAY LIFE

Unlike the eastern mystics who look upon their meditation as an end in itself, we seek to gain from it in our experience of life in our day to day living. How do we bring the effects of Mental Ataraxis into our everyday life? We relax easily enough in the quiet of meditation, but we want more than that; we want to be relaxed in the realities of our day to day existence. We must learn to keep our ease in the face of frustration, provocation, humiliation and pain. This is a simple test of our degree of achievement.

The experience of inner calm in meditation is nothing unless it is reflected in the quality of our life. I have sometimes been criticised for setting a task that is too difficult, for expecting a standard that few if any will attain. I reject this criticism. I believe that in general we accept standards in life which are far too low. It really does not cost us much effort to raise the standard of behaviour that we demand of ourselves. This is one of the fruits of meditation attainable by the ordinary person. It is ripened by practice, and when the time comes it is truly sweet to the taste.

By practising mental relaxation in circumstances of discomfort we train our mind to be at ease when we are faced with the discomforts of daily life. This is something quite different from the various toughening up procedures such as are used in the services for training commandoes, and in some youth training organisations which aim to develop character. In these courses the participants are brought to experience discomfort. For those involved it is very uncomfortable and it hurts. But the body and mind learn to adapt to the discomfort, and as a result the individual comes to be able to carry out his duty in the face of discomfort in a way that would otherwise be impossible. It is essentially an unpleasant toughening up process, and in becoming tougher the individual loses some of his sensitivity, and in this respect is reduced as a human being. This form of training involves quite different physiological and psychological adjustments from those involved in the transcendence of discomfort through meditative experience.

In learning how to transcend the discomforts of daily life

through meditative experience we do not have to tolerate any unpleasantness, discomfort or hurt at all. Unlike the toughening up technique it is a painless process; and, unlike the toughening up technique, it does not involve the individual in the loss of sensitivity.

Toughening up processes involve the hardening of the body and the dulling of the mind, whereas the meditative approach involves the use of our mind in slightly different fashion. In the meditative approach the individual experiences only potential discomfort while in toughening up regimes he has to learn to endure real discomfort.

The potential discomfort for the meditative setting can be provided by different means as the individual wishes. Posture, cold, skin clips or lying on a rough surface can all be used without any feeling of discomfort. We have already discussed the importance of meditating in situations of minor discomfort in order to enhance the meditative process. It is a continuation of this same procedure which brings us to transcend the discomforts of ordinary life.

We can assume any posture which induces slight discomfort. We let our mind relax, and the discomfort has gone. We now continue our meditation in this posture in perfect ease. Squatting cross-legged is a very satisfactory posture as for most people this is slightly uncomfortable. Older people may find that sitting on a hard chair is sufficient. If you should find that you are making yourself endure discomfort, there is something wrong. Either you have not yet learned to let your mind relax, in which case you need a little more practice in this respect; or you may have been too enthusiastic and set yourself in a posture of too great discomfort for your present skill in meditation.

Cold can be used as an effective source of discomfort. I have mentioned that meditating naked gives an increased sense of freedom and naturalness. There is discomfort in the feeling of cold. Then we let our mind relax and the feeling of discomfort has gone. In winter I have used a similar approach by quietly floating in the cold water of a swimming pool.

A paper clip, clothes peg or surgeon's towel clip can be used to pinch the skin and so induce discomfort. But our mind relaxes and there is no discomfort, and our meditation proceeds.

Similarly we can lie on a rough surface. We can use the bathroom floor with a few small objects such as a nail brush or an ashtray under the back, or in summer lying in a bathing gown on the rough surface of the garden patio is satisfactory.

The means of producing the discomfort is immaterial. The

important factor is that the transcendence of minor discomfort in this way not only makes the meditative process more complete, but also has the effect of bringing us to cope with the discomforts of ordinary life without loss of sensitivity.

By practising mental relaxation in the face of continuing distractions we come to be less worried by distracting influences in our ordinary life. When we are first learning how to meditate we assume a comfortable posture. It is only when we have learned something of it that we attempt increasingly uncomfortable postures. It is the same with distracting influences. At first we practise in a quiet place. Then when we have learned how to do it, we practise amid distracting influences, particularly of noise.

In meditating outside, the wind becomes a distracting influence. It blows in our face and ruffles our hair, but we are undisturbed. Flies and insects may buzz about us and crawl on our face. We are only vaguely aware of them, insignificant in the depth of our awareness of the stillness within us.

By mental relaxation in the face of sudden unexpected stimuli, we come to a state of mind in which we do not over-react to sudden unexpected stimuli in ordinary life. In the process of evolution man is developing an increasingly sensitive nervous system. This is good. It makes possible the achievement of new heights of human experience. But of necessity it carries with it one great disadvantage. The more sensitive our nervous system, the more likely we are to over-react to stimuli. We over-react physically. When driving our car, if we see sudden danger we tend to brake or swerve too quickly and too much. We over-react intellectually by making too quick decisions on information that at first seems very good or very bad. We also over-react emotionally by sudden infatuations or hates not only with people but also with things and ideas.

There are many simple ways in which we can arrange to meditate and at the same time experience sudden unexpected stimuli. One of my most successful experiments in this area was meditating in a bathing gown on the lawn in summer just within range of a slowly revolving sprinkler. Every now and then I would suddenly find myself showered with big icy cold drops of water. Similarly on a windy day when meditating under a willow tree the long pendant branches would suddenly be blown across my face. At first the cold water of the sprinkler or the smack on the face from the willow branch would not only interrupt my meditation, but would cause some involuntary muscular response. But I soon reached the stage when these sudden stimuli had little or no effect either on the way of physical response or interfering with my meditation. At the same time I noticed that I had less tendency to over-react to sudden unexpected stimuli, either physical, intellectual or emotional in real life situations.

More recently I have come upon another very pleasant and effective way in which to experience sudden unexpected stimuli.

At the beach on a hot day I sometimes meditate in bathing trunks on a rock near the water's edge. Every now and then with a gust of wind or a larger wave I am suddenly showered with the cold spray. I feel it, of course, but I am in no way disturbed. There is no reaction physically or emotionally, and the ease of mind continues.

We cannot expect to go through life without being confronted with pain. Through our meditative practice we can learn to experience pain without hurt. This is not too difficult and when we have learned to experience pain without hurt we have gained something in the art of living.

From the practical point of view there are four different types of pain. There is pain which we can expect before it occurs such as the pain of minor surgical procedures and examinations, and of course the pain of dental treatment. Then there is sudden unexpected pain which does not give us the chance to prepare ourselves, such as occurs in any accident, great or small, which may befall us. Then there is chronic pain as in cancer, arthritis and other chronic diseases. The fourth type of pain is rather different. It is pain of the mind. Anguish, sorrow, humiliation. Although it is pain of the mind it may distress us and hurt us just as much as pain from injury or disease of our body. We can use slightly different meditative procedures to learn to cope with each of these different types of pain.

We can learn to cope with pain of which we have warning by subjecting ourselves to painful stimuli during our mental relaxation. It is important to remember that this is not an exercise in learning to be tough and teaching ourselves to endure pain. It is the complete opposite of this. We are not being tough and we don't endure any pain. We are completely relaxed in our mind before we subject ourselves to the painful stimulus, so we do not experience pain at all. Beyond the practical use of this exercise in teaching ourselves how to manage this type of pain, it is of great value in increasing the depth and improving the quality of our meditation.

We use two different psychological reactions in the management of pain. Anxiety alerts the nervous system and so increases our perception of pain. A person who is anxious actually feels more pain. So, by being completely relaxed and at ease before the painful stimulus comes to us, our perception of pain is greatly reduced.

The other psychological mechanism involved is more difficult to explain. It is a matter of letting our mind experience pain in its simplest form. That is just as a signal that something is wrong. We feel the pain. We know it is there. But it is a very simple, primitive, undifferentiated feeling, and without any feeling of hurt whatsoever. It is the experience of painless pain.

Please do not say to yourself, 'I can't understand this. Pain hurts. I know this from my ordinary experience of life.' Certainly pain hurts if we have our mind working in its ordinary, alert fashion, but we can, in fact, have our mind work in another way in which we can still feel the pain, but it simply does not hurt. Do not doubt me. I have learned to do it myself quite easily so that I have now had four teeth extracted at different times without discomfort. More importantly, I have shown many others how to do it.

We must come to accept pain as a natural experience of life. In order to learn to control pain we must experiment a little in a completely natural way with minor painful stimuli. Without this experimentation we become too theoretical and divorced from the urgent practical problem of coping with pain when it should come to us. The naturalness of the experimentation is important, so that it does not involve us in any emotion at all, neither fear nor excitement.

I have found that a piece of burning string is the most convenient stimulus with which to learn the control of pain. The procedure is quite simple. Different types of string burn differently. We need string that will burn with a red hot glow and without any actual flame. At first experiment with thin string as thick string gives a correspondingly more severe stimulus. Sometimes it is possible to unravel a piece of thick string and use only a few of the strands of which it is made up.

If you are right-handed roll up the sleeve of your left arm. Have the string and some matches handy or much better a lighted candle. Get comfortable and have a practice run at deep mental relaxation. Then keeping as relaxed as you can, light the string. Very relaxed. Eyes are just sufficiently opened to let you see what you are doing. You feel the relaxation of your face and your forehead. As you feel this relaxation you gently touch the skin of your forearm with the burning tip of the string. It is all very natural. Easily, gently, quietly, unhurriedly, but firmly. All the time feeling our face relaxed. Forehead relaxed. Eyes so relaxed they are almost closed. Just open enough to see the red of the string on the skin of our arm. Let it rest on the skin for a moment, then withdraw it. Slowly. Easily. Then again. This time more firmly. Always keeping the relaxation of the mind. Feeling it in the face, and the eyes almost closed.

Learning to manage sudden unexpected pain. Our general meditative experience helps us in this as it reduces our tendency to over-react. Training in this specific area really requires the help of an assistant. When we are meditating the assistant can sit quietly at our side, and without any warning touch us on the arm with the burning string. If we meditate in a bathing gown, the burning string can be used on any part of the body, and the unexpected quality of the stimulus is increased. Instead of using the burning string, the meditator can be sharply struck on the back with a stick or cane. Unexpected pain can also be produced by suddenly pinching the skin of the meditator. In all these procedures there must be a considerable lapse of time between the stimuli otherwise they are no longer unexpected.

The control of chronic pain is a great step forward in the art of living. It is attained by learning to control artificially induced pain of some duration. People who are suffering chronic pain who read this are likely to react by saying, 'I have enough pain already. I don't want any more artificially induced pain.' Let me explain. The artificially induced pain will not worry you because you will be relaxed and there will be no hurt in it. The important factor is this. It is much easier for your mind to learn to control a new pain rather than start on the old pain with which you have been struggling for so long.

We can use the string again. Start with a thin piece as we want a slow steady burning of the skin, and at first you will not want too strong a stimulus. Use the inside of your forearm as the hairs on the outer side prevent the string lying flat on the skin. You need a pair of scissors close at hand. Then, very relaxed as before. Light the string. Feeling the relaxation in your face. Eyes so relaxed they are half closed. We let the burning string rest on our forearm. Utterly relaxed, we take up the scissors and cut the string about half an inch from the burning end. Deeply relaxed, we wait for the half inch of string to burn. We feel it. Feel it, but there is no hurt in it. We may smell the skin burning. But there is no hurt in it. Then we are aware that the string has burnt out. Finished.

As we become more experienced we repeat the procedure with longer pieces of string of two or three inches. The painful stimulus now lasts for two or three minutes or more. But there is still no pain. Aware that we are being burnt. Yes. But there is no hurt in it. As we come to do it more easily we can increase the intensity of the stimulus by using thicker string. Remember that the string must lie flat on the skin. If it is held off the skin by hairs or by a kink in the string, we do not receive the full stimulus. By this procedure our mind learns how to manage pain of some duration. People with chronic pain who practise this find that the intensity and hurt of their pain is reduced.

An alternative method is to lie on a hard surface with sharp pebbles under the back. If this method is used, there is one important proviso. We must never get up from our painful situation because the pain is hurting us. We aim to do it without the experience of pain. So at first we do not lie on the pebbles for too long. If by chance we should find some pain coming through, we relax more completely, and it is only when the pain has gone again that we get up. We only stop when we are free of pain, never on account of it.

What of pain of the mind, of anguish, sorrow, humiliation, guilt? Pain of the mind comes in many guises. Meditation shows us ease of mind, and we can cope with these problems too. First let us remember that pain of our body is something good and useful. It warns us of some injury or disorder. It serves a useful purpose. That is why in our meditative practice we do not attempt to abolish pain, we only take the hurt out of it. Fear warns us of physical danger. Guilt warns us that we have done wrong. Some of the other pains of the mind are more complex in nature but they have all been evolved as means of helping us. When we are humiliated we are reduced in status. The unpleasant feeling of humiliation makes us think poorly of ourselves. By thinking poorly of ourselves we are better able to accept the reduced status which humiliation involves. So in this way the mental pain of humiliation serves a useful purpose. Sorrow reminds us of our loss, whereas in anguish our sense of loss is so much the more acute.

Doctors try to relieve pain of the mind, whereas some philosophers say we should learn to endure it as part of our human condition. The medical approach is that any pain of the mind, in fact any suffering, should be promptly relieved. Hence the widespread use of tranquillisers, antidepressants and sedative drugs. We do not want people to suffer unnecessarily, but on the other hand we do not want people to live a second class existence with their perception and feelings dulled with an ever-increasing need for drugs. The other approach is that suffering helps us to understand, and we should be prepared to accept it as it comes. A third approach is that of the traditional Hindus and Buddhists who believe that suffering is only avoided through non-attachment.

Through meditative practice we can learn to experience mental pain without the hurt of suffering. Please let yourself come along with me about this, both in the idea of it and the doing of it.

Let us take some simple examples. We have done something wrong, our tax returns are not quite truthful, an affair in which we have let down the other party, an extra-marital pregnancy, any of the incidents of life, past or present, great or small about which we feel guilty. Some theologians hold that we should suffer to expiate our guilt. Most psychiatrists hold that we should not feel guilty at all. But surely we should not destroy ourselves by suffering so that we lose our capacity for a full and useful life participating in the human experience. On the other hand, surely we should retain our sense of guilt as a guide for our future conduct of life in general. I believe that we should strive for a state of mind in which our sense of guilt is preserved but at the same time does not involve destructive suffering.

We can apply similar lines of arguments to other varieties of mental pain. Take sorrow. The mental pain of loss. We have lost someone dear to us, or maybe it is something, tangible or intangible, perhaps it is the loss of someone who once loved us. Let us experience our sense of loss, but let us do so without the hurt of suffering which reduces our capacity for living. I believe that these are things we must aim to achieve.

How can we take the hurt from mental pain? So far we have been theorising. But it is only doing that counts.

The suffering, the hurt of mental pain involves turmoil of our mind. Without turmoil of the mind there is little suffering, little hurt. If our mind is calm, if it is still, suffering ceases. This is how meditative experience can relieve our suffering and take the hurt out of mental pain.

There are two aspects to the relief of mental suffering by meditative experience. If a person is beset with mental pain, he can relieve his suffering by learning how to meditate and then practising it. The turmoil gradually goes from his mind, and the hurt of the mental pain is no longer there. I have seen this happen with many, many people, so I know beyond all doubt that it is effective.

The other aspect of the relief of mental pain concerns those who are already experienced meditators prior to the onset of the mental pain. With these people the hurt of mental pain never really develops. I have had many patients tell me that they have recently been through some terrible experience, being jilted, an extra-marital pregnancy, the disgrace of some member of the family or simple loss of fortune and bankruptcy, and they have coped with the situation in a way that they had not believed possible. In other words the calm of mind from their meditative experience had prevented the usual turmoil of mental pain ever developing.

Remember that the relief of suffering through meditative practice does not involve the logical aspects of the mind. We have grown to rely too much on our logical abilities to the exclusion of other functions of our mind. Many of those who are seen to be suffering are continually advised by well-meaning friends. These people do not understand that their logical advice is of little or no help at all. 'This is something that you have done. It is now in the past. Don't keep worrying about it. Forget about it.' All very logical. But it does not help the suffering one in the least. Similarly, 'She has left you. She has made it clear that she no longer loves you. It is pointless to go on torturing yourself about it.' Logical advice in this vein only adds to the hurt of his sorrow.

The person who is suffering mental pain often tends to reject help through meditative experience. 'How can meditating put right what I have done wrong?' Of course it can't. But it can relieve the hurt of suffering so that we can get on with the business of living. Similarly, 'Meditating can't bring her back'. No, but it can help *us* back to normal life. These matters are obvious to the observer, but the one who is suffering thinks only of his guilt or his loss. We must persuade him to give it a trial.

Then there is another level of rejection. 'Yes, I feel calmer and better while I am meditating, but when I stop, it all returns.' Of course it takes a little while for the effects of the meditative experience to seep into our ordinary life. The meditator can be reassured by being reminded of the fact that he *did* feel more at ease for a short time after the meditative experience. With a little practice the post-meditative calm becomes longer and longer until it becomes part of our ordinary life.

The quality of our life is directly influenced by the way in which we bring the effects of our Mental Ataraxis into our way of living. It is not sufficient to read about it or to think about it or even to practise it. The only thing that counts is living it. To live the effect of the experience is to let it be part of us.

We can live the effect of it, and still engage in a fully active life. This is an essential part of the philosophy which I am offering. There is no withdrawal from life, no isolating ourselves from our fellows, no tendency towards a hermit's life. We aim for full participation in all the practical reality of life, but at the same time retain our ease of mind.

We bring the feeling of calm and ease which we experience during our practice into all aspects of our life. We have the feeling of it as we walk down the street. Good feeling. The ease of our mind and the ease of our inner self. It is reflected in the way we walk. There is ease about it. The rhythm and the naturalness. And because of the ease in ourselves, we perceive things with ease. The people in the street, the expression on their faces and the inner meaning of it. The light and shade, the bustle of the street. We perceive it all with an added vividness because of our own ease.

It is the same at work. We are at ease in ourselves, so we do it with less effort. We cope with people at work better because we are no longer annoyed by what they say or do. We have gained understanding and we no longer over-react as we have in the past.

It is the same at home. We are at ease in ourselves, and the irritability which did so much to spoil our home life has passed from us.

I have the habit of jotting down some of the exact words the patient says to me. In each case I have done this when the patient first came in, prior to the relaxing meditation, not after it. This is quite important as the patient's assessment of things immediately after the session may be distorted by the calm which lingers on after the meditative experience. Most of the phrases recorded from patients whom I have not seen for at least a week, and more often a month, confirm my most enthusiastic hopes for each and my complete faith in Mental Ataraxis as a method that will bring ease wherever it is properly applied.

At first we bring ourselves to use a conscious act of mind to experience the effects of it in our everyday life. We keep reminding ourselves of the way we felt during our periods of practice and in the moments immediately afterwards. More than reminding ourselves. We make a conscious effort to prolong the calm which follows our periods of practice. And in our daily life we bring ourselves to recapture it. It comes to us, momentarily at first, then for longer periods, and we soon find that we are experiencing periods of calm and ease in our ordinary life which we had not known before.

We can facilitate the advent of the experience into our daily life by recalling bodily feelings which come to us during our practice. For instance, when we practise we commonly feel the relaxation of the muscles of our face. Our forehead smooths out, and we are aware of the relaxation of the muscles around our eyes and mouth. Now, when we walk down the street, we can again bring ourselves to feel the same relaxation of our face. We feel the smoothing out of our forehead, deeply, and we experience it in the calm of our mind. It is easy to do this as we walk down the street. As we become more adept at it, we find that we can do it just as easily while we are about our ordinary tasks at work and at home. In this way we bring the experience of our practice into our daily life and gain from it in all the aspects of our living.

We soon come to the stage when the ease of it is there with us, without any conscious effort on our part at all. When this comes, and it comes very much sooner than most people at first expect, we have, in fact, added a new dimension to the quality of our life. We just do things easily and naturally in a way which we did not think possible before.

People who practise it but who make no conscious effort to bring the experience into their daily life are still benefited in this way. It seeps through into their daily life without their being aware of it. But it takes longer. So I would strongly advise you to make this conscious effort to initiate the effect into your daily life.

My evidence for this rests on experience with patients who have come to me seeking the relief of some specific psychosomatic symptom. Some of these have been people who profess no interest in such matters as the quality of life. They want relief of their symptoms and that is all. Because they want relief they are quite prepared to practise Mental Ataraxis. But, because they have no interest in these other aspects of life, they make no attempt to bring the effects of the experience into their ordinary living. Nevertheless, I have seen many such people whose way of life has changed for the better as a side effect of their learning how to relieve their psychosomatic symptoms.

We can integrate our whole life on the background of our experience of Mental Ataraxis. One life. A unit. A wholeness. I have seen some who seem to think that it is appropriate to be relaxed when they practise, and equally appropriate to be tense when they are at work. There can be no separate compartments to our life. Our ease of mind pervades all that we do, our home life, our life at work and our leisure life. It pervades it all because it is part of our inner self.

In bringing the effect of it into our daily life, we still retain our capacity for decisive action. This of course is of vital importance. I have had people who have not understood, say to me, 'Do you want me to go about in a kind of trance?' Let us be quite clear about this. When we are practising we are, in fact, in a kind of trance because we are no longer aware of the things around us. We aim to bring the effects of this state into our daily life – the effects of it, not the state itself. We want to capture and keep the calm and ease of mind which we learn in this way. We can do this and still retain our capacity for decisive action. In fact, this capacity is increased through the reduction of our anxiety so that we can now use the whole of our mental energy in decisive action, whereas in the past we have had to use a significant part of it in controlling our anxiety.

As we bring it into our daily life we come to do difficult and un-pleasant tasks and at the same time remain at ease in ourselves. In other words we no longer over-react to situations. We are at ease when we are doing easy things, but we are also at ease when we are doing difficult things. And because we are at ease, we do them so much the better. And in so doing we attain a greatly improved way of life.

PART TWO

The Discipline of Ease

The Fruits of Mental Ataraxis
The Practical Ordering of our Material Life

8

WHAT WE DO AND WHAT WE ARE

As a psychiatrist I have had greater opportunity than most people of observing what it is that has contributed to the good life of some, and of observing those things which have destroyed the hopes of so many others. It is the story of life; it is the story of us all.

Our *doing*, whether at work, at home or at our leisure activities, is intimately related to what we are. In fact, in doing what is psychologically and philosophically appropriate to our individual self we are the better for it. This much is simple, but immediately there comes the problem of our own individuality. What are we?

As individuals we are the sum total of our habitual psychological reactions for it is in this that we display our own unique qualities which make us the individual that we are. Inasmuch as these are our defences against anxiety, they are not constant in the way that we commonly imagine them to be, so we ourselves are subject to change. What is still more important is the fact that these changes in the nature of our defences can be initiated by our own volition. So we are not fixed in what we are. For instance, we are different now from what we were in our childhood. I am not referring to our physical growth, but to the changes in our psychological reactions and our sense of values.

We are still capable of further change, but, by and large, we resist it because we have either grown comfortable in our habitual defences or are too frightened to move from them. By first considering what we do as we are at present, the subsequent changes in ourself will come about so much more easily. We are better when what we do satisfies various materialistic, biological, psychological, philosophical and spiritual reactions within us. This is the crux of the question as to what we should do in life. We shall attempt to evaluate different aspects of our life from this point of view.

We are living beings in a world of reality and to deny our material needs is to deny our biological heritage. Any philosophy or way of life which would deny this basic ingredient of our make-up must of necessity fail. But the thread of our material need is closely woven with our ethical and spiritual striving. For instance, we have within us a biological drive to provide the material needs for our mate and our offspring and others dear to us. Even in this simple matter, material living and ethical experience are closely linked. This is our destiny. It is something bred into us. In this respect the philosophy of withdrawal and meditation fails as it denies this drive which is part of us. So does the hippie philosophy that life is for living with the satisfaction of simple pleasures. It denies the idea of working to provide the material needs of those dependent upon us. Those who would advocate our withdrawal from competitive life are finding quite wide support in these times of increased stress, but this is a philosophy which denies a basic element of our being. We must work to satisfy our material needs. We cannot escape into the delusion that they do not exist. At the same time, we must not allow our material needs to overshadow other equally compelling needs within us. This, of course, has become the great error of the materialistic society in which we live.

The pursuit of material needs is becoming less biologically important. During the long history of our evolutionary development different aspects of our being have changed in their importance to us. For example, physical muscular strength is no longer so important to us as it was in the earlier stages of our development. So, also, with aggression. In primitive times the ability to be aggressive may have been lifesaving, but now it is more likely to lead us into trouble. On the other hand, our intellectual abilities are becoming increasingly important to us. If we apply this principle to our material needs, we immediately see that they are becoming less and less important. At an early stage of our development they occupied most of our life. But now they need take up only a small part of it. We must remember this as we are prone to continue in our old patterns of doing things, and we tend to cling to value systems which we should have outgrown.

Although our material needs are now less biologically important, they have become increasingly socially important. This is something which we cannot just dismiss. We compete against our fellows. Those in the past who competed more successfully had a better chance of survival and a better chance of rearing offspring. So we compete. In the past this often brought us to fight with our fellows. Now we do this in symbolic fashion, and the breathlessness of my hard-fought tennis yesterday reactivated ridicule. 'Fancy Dad as a painter'. 'Mum can bake her pottery my inherited sense of combat.

In a similar way we compete with our fellows through material gain. When we move up another rung in the hierarchy of the business firm we gain more than increase in salary. We have achieved something. We have had a win; and with it comes status which extends beyond our immediate job in the firm. In this way we compete with our fellows. If you are young, material success still brings the chance of a more desirable mate. If you are older, material success brings with it increased social status. However unpalatable this may be to us, it is in fact true.

The need to compete with our fellows is part of us. In the past we have fought physically, now we compete by material gain, and we get the edge on the other fellow just as we did when we knocked him down in the past. When we look at it like this, we can see that this type of competition by material gain should, in fact, be unnecessary. It is a low level life style; but we are what we are, and we have this need within us.

However we shall see that we can change. It need be just a little change – just another step in our evolutionary progress – and this style of intense materialistic competition is no longer necessary to us. We then have time for simple pleasures, and also for the pleasure of using our mind. This is a newer form of satisfaction as opposed to the more primitive satisfaction of material gain. We can use our mind to think, but more importantly, we can come to use it to experience the inner reality as well as the outer reality of material things; and by arranging what we do in life in a way that gives scope for these experiences, we ensure that our life becomes so much the better for us.

We are not what we seem to be. Through our unconscious attempts to cope with our inner anxiety we have become a distortion of what we really are. We are two different things at the same time, the caricature and the real. To understand ourselves we must resolve this apparent paradox.

For the most part, we see ourselves and others as the caricature. This is how we are in the reality of our daily lives. Yet sometimes, just occasionally, in some moment of stress, love or anguish, or in the moment of an encounter when we meet another in complete unguardedness, or at times of communion with our deity or nature itself, we see ourselves and others in a new light of deeper reality. The distortion has gone. We see through the veil of caricature, and a vision of the deeper self emerges.

But we must be clear about this. The metaphor gives only partial understanding. The distortions are not just an illusion or a facade with the true self lying beneath. We are, in fact,

the distorted person. This is as we are in the life that we live.
At the same time we are this other thing, natural, open and
human in the full sense of the word. This is the paradox of life.

We feel that we are what our personality is. We feel that our
personality which gives us our own unique identity is the real
essence of our true self. We experience our personality as
intensely our own, as the very core of our being. Other things
that are part of us may change. We may grow fat or thin; we
may lose a leg or an eye, but our personality remains intact.
This is what we like to believe. But, in reality, our personality
is only the sum of all our defences against anxiety. As such it is
not nearly as consistent and enduring as we like to believe.

To be introvert or extravert is merely to say that one favours
particular approaches to life that reduce anxiety, one by withdrawal from material living and preoccupation with the inner
life, and the other by concentrating on practical reality and
avoiding the inner life. Each in his own way reduces anxiety by
his own particular approach. Similarly, the perfectionist attempts
to reduce his anxiety by trying to have everything just right.
The suspicious person is suspicious because he feels that his
suspicions are a protection to him. The humble and obsequious
reduce anxiety by placating others. The aggressive person feels
that aggression is the best way of protecting himself, while the
timid achieve the same end by avoiding conflict; and so we can
go on enumerating all the various traits of character which
combine to make up our personality. Seen in this perspective,
our personality is merely the sum total of a mass of defensive
psychological reactions.

*With reduction of anxiety the individual's personality characteristics
become less marked.* I have seen this happen many times. The
introvert becomes less introverted, the extravert less extraverted,
the suspicious less suspicious, the obsequious less obsequious,
the perfectionist less encumbered by unnecessary rigidity,
and so on. Perhaps most marked of all is the way in which
habitually aggressive persons become less aggressive as the
level of their anxiety is reduced. In other words our personality
is not fixed and immutable in the way that we feel it to be, but
on the contrary has a fair degree of plasticity even into middle
and old age.

*The reason why most of us fail when we try to make a change
in our personality is that we rely on a logical approach rather*

than the simple reduction of anxiety. The introvert reasons that life would be better if he were not so withdrawn and so occupied with his inner life. But no amount of reasoning will make him change because his condition is maintained as a defence against anxiety. A person may realise that his personality is distorted by suspicion or jealousy, and he may try to amend his attitude, but so long as it serves as a protection against anxiety, he will always fail. On the other hand, if the anxiety is reduced, the defensive distortion of the personality no longer serves any psychological purpose and it gradually recedes.

The natural insecurity of our practical lives produces anxiety which in turn distorts our personality. Strangely enough, it is not easy to isolate our anxieties; even those anxieties of our practical living are not as easy to isolate as we might expect. It is humiliating to feel insecure, so our mind unconsciously comes to our aid to save us from this humiliation. It tricks us into denying that various events of our life make us feel insecure. 'Oh, no. I don't worry about that at all.' Yet, through the thin disguise of our dreams we can often see that we do.

Our mind also uses other ways to save us the humiliation of feeling insecure. Without being aware of what we are doing, we blame our feeling of insecurity on to some other event which is less humiliating. 'Of course I am anxious about my business. With this government you do not know what is going to happen next.' In this way we avoid the humiliation of admitting that our insecurity is due to our own failure to cope with the situation. Or nearer to home, if we think of our children, we say to ourselves, 'They are fine. They are all in good jobs', and so deny that they have other problems.

By a further extension of this principle we develop habitual reactions to cope with the anxiety which comes from the insecurity of our practical life. We become withdrawn, suspicious or aggressive or whatever the case may be. It all becomes a part of ourselves, and we live our life as a caricature of what we really are.

But it is not only the insecurity of our practical lives, there is also the insecurity within ourselves which produces anxiety and distorts our personality. Although defensive mechanisms operate to save us the humiliation of being too aware of the uncertainties of practical life, it is not too difficult to understand this source of anxiety. But to understand the insecurity of our inner self is much more difficult. It is an unpleasant subject, so we would prefer to avoid it.

This inner insecurity has various facets. We are uncertain as to what we are. 'What *is* a living being?' So we avoid the worry of it by refusing to think about it.

At a simpler level we are often uncertain as to what it really means to be a man or to be a woman. I have seen many young people beset with insecurity of this nature. Many of them had set out to try to reassure themselves by all manner of practical experimentation, but it had been of no avail because their insecurity is not of the body, but is of the inner self.

I have seen many others whose insecurity has concerned their identity. They keep pondering the question. 'What am I? What am I, really?' Some seek the answer in various forms of mysticism, others in the experience of hallucinogenic drugs, and still others in religion. But for many the anxiety has persisted, distorting their personality into a caricature of what they really are.

To gain maturity we must achieve a synthesis of our two selves; the practical self of reality and the inner self of what we are without the defensive distortions of our personality. You will follow what I mean if you think of some of your friends. You can think of some who have very marked distortions of their personality, and it is hard to imagine what kind of people these would be without these distortions. On the other hand, it is likely that you can think of a few people who have a kind of naturalness about them, an openness. These are people who, in themselves, are less distorted by anxiety. In other words, they are individuals in whom the self of practical life and the inner self are much closer. They are moving towards an integration of their personality which in everyday life we describe as maturity.

Should we try to cope with the stresses of practical living without psychological defences, and so avoid distortion of our personality? As long as we are frail within, we must have psychological defences to protect ourselves. Without defences we would be so hurt, humiliated and angered that our nervous system would be in such a turmoil of activity that we would be unable to manage the ordinary affairs of everyday living. So, as long as we remain frail and insecure within ourselves, psychological defences are a necessity, and the consequent distortion of our personality is inevitable.

The crucial step is the development of inner security. This involves the reduction of anxiety. There are self regulating mechanisms within the mind which can effectively reduce our anxiety if we provide suitable circumstances in which they can operate. This can be done quite easily and naturally in the practise of relaxing meditative experience. Our anxiety is reduced and our defensive reactions lose their intensity, and the distortions of our personality become so much the less.

For mature living we need more than the reduction of anxiety — we need to understand as well. We might think that if we work to gain understanding, then our anxiety will cease; that in a way our anxiety is a result of our failure to understand. This is an attractive intellectual proposition, but it is not the way it happens. As a result of over thirty years experience in psychiatry, I have learned that anxiety inhibits our understanding. In face of the defences and distortions of the personality maintained by anxiety, true understanding is impossible.

However, if we first reduce our anxiety by relaxing meditative experience, then understanding of the deeper nature of our being can come to us. In particular, we can gain some sense of our true identity, of the meaning of our sexuality, of our relationship between the realistic and spiritual value systems within us, and of our place in the natural order of things. With a greater degree of understanding we are consequently more secure and less sullied by distortions of our personality. We have in fact started on the road to maturity.

9

OUR LIFE AT WORK

A satisfactory way of life at work involves more than a good wage, good conditions, security, holidays and superannuation. It involves other things – intangibles. Because they are intangible we are inclined to let them slide, ignore them, forget about them. Furthermore, these intangibles about our work are vaguely worrying to us. When we do come to discuss them with our inner self, it often seems that we do not come out of the discussion too well. We try to escape from problems that we cannot manage very well. We pretend that they do not exist and, in this case, we come back to evaluating our job in the materialistic terms which we cope with so much more easily.

We show an extraordinary lack of concern about the deeper consequences of our occupation. Of course the boy or girl on leaving school is not sufficiently experienced in life to understand the consequences of his choice of job. He sees mainly the short term effects, pay, bonus, and weekends free from work. And if he does look seriously at the more distant effects he often sees them in terms of glamorised status. This is all understandable. The young person, boy or girl, lacks experience and is reluctant to accept parental advice in such matters. But it is strange that the experienced adult when faced with the necessity or opportunity of a change of occupation should so frequently assess the situation in the same superficial way as teenagers.

The product of what we do in our work has its effect on others, and this in turn has an inward effect on ourselves. We may be engaged in work which is inherently valueless or even harmful. If we are engaged in selling or advertising some inferior product, it is clear that we are being debased by our work. Even more so, if what we are doing is actively harmful, such as work connected with the manufacture or sale of cigarettes, it tends to destroy us morally.

So we thence evolve simple psychological defences which help us escape any feeling of responsibility for the consequences of our work. 'It's only a job.' 'I just work for the money and that is all there is to it.' 'That's their responsibility, it has nothing to do with me.' 'A man must work to support his wife and kids, you can't be too choosy about it.' 'If I didn't have this job, someone else would.' 'If people buy the rotten things, it is really none of my business.' We are all familiar with these trite attitudes. They really go to show that the person who says these things is, in fact, disturbed at the meaninglessness of his way of life.

It is not just the working man who has to say these things to escape from his inner disquiet. Those at a higher level have the same need to escape responsibility but, it is expressed in slightly different terms. 'We must think of the shareholders. It is only honest to think of our shareholders.'

There is an important question that frequently arises. Is it only women with their capacity for childbearing and ability to influence the very young who are capable of a truly rewarding way of life? In terms of innate biology woman has something which man can never have. Indeed, man has been aware of this, and over the centuries has tried to compensate by giving emphasis to that which he has and which is so obviously lacking in woman. So from the biological point of view it would seem that woman does have a more directly rewarding way of life open to her than has man.

However, woman now looks to horizons beyond the home. She sees the glitter of high wages, intellectual participation and the means of acquiring electrical gadgetry without end. It would seem that woman is halted at the crossroads of two opposing ways of life; but it need not be like this. In our psychological and sociological evolution the New Woman will come to see that she is able to fulfil her feminine role in life and at the same time participate in all that is going on around her. In this way she can achieve a synthesis of outer reward and inner satisfaction.

We must not evaluate the worth of our work on a too moralistic basis. The comedian and the prostitute may also contribute. If the comedian relies for his laughs on ridiculing the finer aspects of life he debases both his audience and himself. But the comedian who can bring us to laugh by emphasising our inherent foibles helps reduce the tension that we have within us and at the same time bring us some insight into ourselves.

There is no need to emphasise the generally debasing effects of prostitution. But I recollect very well seeing one of these girls as a patient. She was sensitive, intuitive, understanding. True, she took money, and shared her body with married men. She talked about these things. From what she said I believe that men were often uplifted rather than debased through their contact with her. So let us not use too rigid criteria of worth for the work that we do.

Perhaps it is our attitude rather than the work we do which counts. I am a doctor, and I know that medicine can often be an inwardly fulfilling way of life for those who seek it. And it can also be a very remunerative way of life. It is clear that this aspect of things has the power to debase some of those who practise medicine. What can be uplifting to one can be degrading to another. But the degraded one does not think of it like this. He is protected from such disturbing thoughts either by his insensitivity or by active psychological defences. 'Medicine is no different from anything else. It is simply a business like any other job. You get what you can from the customer.'

Work that is associated with nature is inwardly fulfilling in a way that other work is not. The farmer complains of the bad weather and the low price for his products. But he does not want to change his way of life. No. Not for anything.

None of us is very clear about our sense of inner fulfilment or otherwise, and the farmer least of all. But these things have a psychological explanation. Over the countless generations of our development as human beings we have had bred into us all manner of psychological reactions which have been of advantage to the individual and to the race as a whole. Thus those of us in the past who have felt some inner satisfaction in sowing the seed and seeing it grow have been better farmers. They have been more successful and have had more surviving offspring. So this quality of mind has become part of us. By dint of his occupation, the farmer has the opportunity to experience this inner satisfaction which is denied those who work on the industrial conveyor belt.

Work that has some biological relevance brings a sense of inner fulfilment similar to the sense of fulfilment achieved from working on the land. In the remote past, those who obtained some satisfaction in tending the young, were better at it, and had more surviving children. So the sense of fulfilment in caring for the young, in mothering and in teaching, has become part of our biological inheritance; hence the inner fulfilment of those who work in these fields.

The same principle extends into many areas. It has been biologically advantageous to us as a race if we obtained inner satisfaction in helping the sick and needy. So any present day occupation which concerns the sick and needy brings with it these satisfactions of the past. In considering this we must be clear that this type of satisfaction is in the nature of an inherited disposition and is independent of any moral, ethical or religious satisfaction which may also accrue from such work.

In evaluating our life's work by its sociological effect on our family or the community at large we are still using a materialistic way of judging things. Although it is materialistic, it would seem to be valid. If, through our work, we contribute something towards making life better for those around us, it would seem that our life's work must be worthwhile. Yet there may be other levels at which the situation can be judged which are equally valid, but which are much more difficult to appraise such as our affect on others as we go about our work. Some people cast a shadow, and we feel the gloom of it when we are near them. Some stir, and in their stirring of others bring discontent to the surface. Some others radiate light, and while we are in their company we too are illuminated so that we no longer think or feel or do those darker things which so often come to us.

Our work must satisfy the basic orientation of our personality. It must suit our mind, just as it must suit our body. A physically weak person is not suited to heavy labouring work, nor is a dullard suited for high grade work of the intellect; but it is much more complicated than this. The minds of different people work in rather different ways. This is largely determined by their general attitude to the world. This in turn is really a product of their habitual ways of avoiding anxiety. We are better when our work brings us to use our mind in the particular way in which we are accustomed to using it.

The extravert needs a job which concerns the practical realities of life and one which brings him or her into contact with others. We have all evolved different ways of managing our anxiety through our general approach to life. The extravert concerns himself with practical things and finds greatest satisfaction in life through contact with friends.

We can see that in the past these characteristics have been of great biological value. Those who were practical in their approach to life had a better chance of survival, and so also were those who had plenty of friends who in time of need would come to their aid.

Those who have this approach to life need work which satisfies these aspects of their personalities. To them, life in other areas seems lacking in something because they are unable to obtain these inner satisfactions from it.

The introvert needs work in which he uses his natural sensitivity, thoughtfulness and idealism. The extravert is concerned with the practical reality of material things, whereas the introvert tends to concern himself with the inner reality of his thoughts and feelings. This is an advance from the more primitive approach when our sole concern had to be with practical material things in order to survive. But the introvert approach also has some biological value. By withdrawal we escape physical danger and also the danger of anxiety from difficult social contact with others. And by withdrawal we can think and get things into proper perspective. Introverts need these satisfactions, and they need a way of life in which they can find them in their everyday occupation.

We live in a world of practical reality in which we have to earn a living. I have seen many young people whose preoccupation with their inner life has led them to neglect this basic fact. 'I shall live by writing poetry.' 'I shall sell my paintings.' 'I shall get a grant and study philosophy.' This is the talk of the young introvert, sensitive, idealistic and completely lacking his brother extravert's way of looking at the practical aspects of life. Without realistic provision for his material needs, the idealistic young introvert's way of life soon deteriorates.

The usual story, as I have heard it so often, is one of increasingly poor nutrition, increasing use of drugs, and a gradual falling off of creative ability. The answer, of course, is a part time job, and part time artistic activity until he is established in a way of life.

The obsessive, perfectionistic person needs a job in which he can use his innate thoroughness to advantage and so gain inner satisfaction. From the biological point of view it is easy to see how the quality of thoroughness has helped us survive; but it also has a psychological effect. Just as the withdrawal of the introvert is used as a defence against anxiety, the obsessive uses his thoroughness as a similar defence. Inwardly, this individual feels that if or she can have everything just right there can be nothing to worry about.

So those of us who have this trait of personality need work in which we can indulge our thoroughness and at the same time be rewarded by this feeling of inner satisfaction. And of course these biological and psychological satisfactions are distinct from the logical and moralistic satisfaction of having done a good job.

Hysteric, enthusiastic, compassionate, aggressive and suspicious persons can all find occupations which give an outlet for these traits of personality. The dramatic hysteric finds satisfaction in the performing arts. The enthusiast is a born salesman because enthusiasm, like other emotions, is catching and their clients unconsciously take on their enthusiasm. Social work in various forms gives scope for our feelings of compassion. The aggressive person often finds a niche in some area of law enforcement, and suspicious people find outlet in work involving inquiry in one form or another.

There is a great diversity of personality traits which we can use to advantage in our work. Passive traits in our personality allow us to cope with matters which we cannot control, and so suit us to subordinate jobs which do not involve too much initiative or authority. On the other hand people who are basically aggressive find satisfaction in work which involves the use of authority. Warm-hearted people have their own particular job satisfactions. Warm-heartedness, like these other traits, is a way of coping with life. In primitive times the warm-hearted had more friends, so were less likely to come to harm. If we are warm hearted, people like us and our anxiety is reduced. Others find close contact with their fellows to be threatening and unconsciously defend themselves with an emotionally cold attitude of mind which makes them better suited for work with things rather than people.

Sexually aware people use the asset of their sexuality in coping with others. They use a sexual gambit with the opposite sex, and with their own sex often indirectly communicate the idea, 'We are in this together, we understand each other'. This leads to easy interpersonal relations and suits the individual for receptionist or personnel work.

Although these personality traits are really defensive distortions of our personality, we can use them to our advantage in the work that we do. This is the pragmatic approach. Our personality traits are imperfections. If we were really mature we would live our lives in real naturalness without any of these distortions. We are beset with something which is basically imperfect, but by finding ourselves the right kind of work we can in fact use our imperfection as an asset.

As we gain greater ease in ourselves there is less need to suit our work so closely to our personality. By reducing the level of our anxiety through a more mature attitude to life, aided by relaxing meditative experience, these distortions of our personality become less marked as they are no longer maintained by the same pressure of anxiety. We have greater freedom. We are more mature, and we are at liberty to choose our work from a wide area of interests rather than being forced into certain jobs on account of our particular traits of personality.

Our work should be consistent with our individual balance between dependence and independence. This concerns the degree to which we are supervised at work. It comes about this way. As children we were all dependent on our parents and other adults around us. In early times those who did not accept some degree of dependence and guidance were less likely to survive. This need for dependence and guidance continues into adult life to varying degree. So different people need different degrees of supervision in the form of someone to whom they can turn at work. It is easy to see this in the different ways in which factory workers look to the foreman. But exactly the same psychological reaction occurs in slightly disguised form in the highest echelons of big business management.

The child is dependent on his parents, but as he grows into adulthood he strives to become independent. This step of complete psychological independence is, in fact, never attained as we all live our lives in a complex of interdependent relationships, but some attain independence to a greater degree than others. Such people are irked by close supervision at work; so also are those who had more than usual difficulty as children in attaining emotional independence from their parents. For these people close supervision produces anxiety and tension by reactivating their childhood problems.

We are better in ourselves when we work in an atmosphere of good morale. This applies equally to the unskilled worker and to the top executive. It means that we should endeavour to work in an area where morale is good. It also means that individually we should contribute to the morale of those about us. In doing this our life is so much the better.

Morale is rather a difficult matter to discuss. For our present purpose I take morale to be that quality of mind which brings us to go beyond the call of duty. In this way, morale would seem to run contrary to the biological interests of the individual. This is something strange indeed, as the psychological reactions which we have so far examined have all been clearly of greater or lesser biological advantage to us. There seems little advantage in doing something for the firm which is not really expected of us and for which we will not be paid or otherwise rewarded. I think this reaction, which we call morale, has its origin in the tribe. When the tribe was called upon to fight, it was the survival of the tribe as a whole rather than that of the individual which was biologically important. The tribe had a better chance of survival if it consisted of individuals of high morale who were prepared to sacrifice themselves for the tribe. So there is a latent tendency within us to act in this way; and, of course, the modern firm, just like the primitive tribe, is more likely to survive if its members have good morale.

Our morale is better when we identify with the institution for which we work. This again is a hangover from our tribal days, but there is an important change in the situation. In primitive times we were very much part of our family, and our family was very much part of the tribe, so morale in the tribe was an integral part of our life. However this has changed. We ourselves are not so integrated with our family and our family, except in rare cases, is not integrated in any way at all with the firm for which we work, so it is more difficult for us to develop morale in our firm than it was within our tribe in the past.

We are better in ourselves when we identify with the firm for which we work. This is a matter of considerable sociological significance in the present day. We are better in ourselves when we experience psychological reactions which were once of biological value to us. We may do this either directly or disguised in symbolic fashion. Our firm has become the modern counterpart of our tribe for which we fought and laboured, and our identification with the firm brings us similar satisfactions.

When the individual goes home and refers to the firm as 'we' he has made this identification; but if he refers to the firm as 'they', there is clearly no identification. The individual who identifies is happier in his work and better in himself. Many socialist leaders miss the importance of this basic psychological trait when they bring employees to dissociate themselves from management, the argument being that by dissociating themselves in this way they are freer to drive a hard bargain about wages and conditions of employment. This is true, and it is all very logical, but in taking on this attitude they lose the significant psychological satisfaction of identifying with those for whom they work.

Work that provides a sense of fellowship helps to satisfy our gregarious needs. This is simple enough. In tribal days we were much safer if we kept in close contact with our fellows. Those who wandered off on their own were likely victims of wild animals or hostile tribesmen. So the feeling of liking to be with our fellows has become a part of our psychological makeup. Expressed like this it would seem to be the result of some kind of reasoned behaviour; but this is not so at all. These very basic reactions came to us before we had evolved much capacity for reason. It was just that over countless generations those who liked to stay with their fellows survived while those who did not perished.

So there has been bred into our race a liking to be with our fellows. This liking has continued with us despite the fact that its protective value has largely come to an end. If the circumstances of our work are such that we can have some pleasant contact with our workmates, this basic need of our personality is satisfied and we are better for it.

Our work must seem meaningful and have some sense of purpose beyond the immediate material rewards. We accept this idea, but only vaguely so, far too vaguely. What are these other rewards? Do they really exist? There are conventional yardsticks by which we can measure our salary, the physical conditions of our work, and our retirement allowances. But how can we measure the sense of purpose which we derive from our life's work? Young people whom I have seen as patients have often said that they would like to work for the United Nations Organisation, or World Health Organisation or, nearer to home, in some job with a clearly defined social significance.

Two men have recently spoken to me like this, one the personnel manager of a large organisation and the other the manager of a prosperous family business. They were both successful, but both were haunted by the idea that their present job did not satisfy something within them which needed to be satisfied if life was to be really worthwhile. One moved to another firm which has given him much freer scope to help the employees, not only with their work but also in personal matters. The other has become extremely active in part time social work.

Again it is common for the successful executive in retirement to devote himself to work on a hospital board. I could name half a dozen of my friends who have done this. The more successful they were as an executive, and the more ruthless, the greater has been their clamour to serve on a hospital board! It is as if in this late stage of their life they are trying to find the fulfilment which eluded them in their life's work.

There is a tendency to evaluate the intangible rewards of our work in terms of social and medical impact. This is too simple, and basically too materialistic. This type of work has become recognised in western society as worthwhile. Accordingly those who work in these areas receive both an inner sense of reward and approval from their fellows.

These criteria are far too shallow. The woman who simply cares for her home and family often makes a far greater contribution. But she needs to be mature and secure in herself or she may be robbed of her inner reward by being too influenced by the social climate of the moment. Similarly the man who sees the reward of his job in his support of his family may experience this as a sense of inner reward. But if his work is socially useful in itself he is then doubly rewarded. But in considering such matters we must not take too narrow a view as to what is socially useful.

We are rewarded in our work if it brings with it a sense of completion. Again this reaction has a biological origin. In the days of our pre-history, those of us who finished the task, gained from what they were doing, and so had a better chance of survival than others. So we have come to like finishing things. This feeling of the satisfaction of completion is with us whatever the job. It is quite distinct from the feeling of relief which comes to us on completing a task when we expect it to be followed by a period of rest or leisure. This of course is one of the reasons why the conveyor belt system of production is so destroying to the human personality. The worker can never say: 'I made it.' This is where the artist and the artisan can gain such satisfaction in their work. Even the doctor can feel, 'There he goes. With the help of God, I got him well.'

We are better for it, if our work demands the full use of our problem-solving ability. 'Oh for an easy job, a soft job.' This is a wish that comes to many of us who work hard. But the soft job palls. Patients say to me, 'There is no challenge in my work, I think I shall get another job'. Only last week an intelligent young woman in a highly paid job in the Public Service said to me, 'I simply can't stand it, the boredom, the boredom, the boredom.' I am sure that many employers of labour would be surprised if they knew how many of their work force felt like this. We are like the youngster who stretches his arms and legs enjoying the feel of the new found strength of his limbs. He needs to flex them. It is similar with the adult. Over millions of years we have developed a brain and have learned how to use it. Life is better when our work gives us reasonable opportunity to do this.

On the other hand, work which produces anxiety in us destroys the quality of our life. There is not only the unpleasant feeling of nervous tension, but anxiety is the cause of all our psychosomatic discomforts and ill health. Perhaps still more importantly, anxiety distorts our personality by motivating us to take on defensive attitudes. In this way we become a lesser person than we might be.

Work which involves ever increasing targets of production increases our anxiety and reduces the quality of our life. I have seen many people with psychosomatic symptoms whose anxiety has been due to their being caught up in this type of situation. Commonly they are sales personnel who are given specific targets which they must attain. It often happens that when these targets are attained they are further increased by the management so that the unfortunate salesman lives a life of increasing nervous tension until he or she finally breaks down. We must remember that salesmen often acquiesce to this way of life, being lured on by greater monetary reward only to find themselves a nervous wreck.

I have seen other people who work with computers caught up in a similar situation. The computer must be kept going. It must never be idle. So it comes about that the machine, like a Frankensteinian monster, sets the pace of those who attend it.

The same principles apply in any factory that works on a conveyor system. The problem is that we all vary in the speed of our reactions. The fast worker experiences little anxiety because he is working well within the limits of his ability. But the slow worker, who may well be a much better worker, has nothing to spare. Some extra stress of no great magnitude, problems with partner or children, or simply some mild infection, may be sufficient to increase his nervous tension so that he can no longer cope with the speed required.

Promotion beyond our capacity may be flattering, but it increases our anxiety. People who have suffered in this way, who have seen me professionally, usually fit into one of three categories.

There are people in family businesses who are appointed to managerial status for family reasons rather than ability. Many of these people have been quite unaware of the cause of their nervous tension. Unconscious processes of the mind cause them to project their troubles on to members of their staff, and they are thus saved the humiliation of being confronted with the fact that they lack the ability to cope with the job.

The second category consists of plausible people. They have the ability to make people like them. They sell themselves well. This is usually not a matter of purposeful contrivance, but is rather the pattern of their life style. Because they are likeable fellows, they get the job over the more able but less likeable person. The plausible and likeable quality of these people is sometimes related to latent homosexual traits which unconsciously influence the employer. The new job of which he is not really capable brings an increase in nervous tension, psychosomatic discomforts and a deterioration in the individual's way of life.

The third group are those who have been very successful executives but who fail when promoted to the responsibility of full management. Of those whom I have seen in this situation, the failure has usually arisen through a characteristic of their personality rather than lack of inherent ability. As children we could always ask mother or father. It was good to have them in the background. With some of us this continues on into adult life. We may still discuss problems with them, or it may be that we unconsciously feel that they are there, and we could fall back on them if need be. When there is someone above us at work we have the same feeling. When our parents die or when we are promoted to a situation with no one above us, the level of our anxiety is likely to increase and our performance at work deteriorates.

Another group of people who often fail when appointed to full managerial responsibility are the obsessives. Their perfectionistic thoroughness and attention to detail make them very successful executives. But their habitual attention to detail restricts their vision. They do not see the big picture, and the good life which they enjoyed as successful subordinates deteriorates in the discomfort of the managerial chair.

Promotion may bring us to areas beyond our cultural background and so cause anxiety. I have seen many people in this situation. It is the story of the self-made man. By dint of sheer ability and hard work he finally finds himself in top management. His contemporaries are better educated, more versed in social graces and more sophisticated in cultural matters than he is. His new position involves him in various social activities. He can cope with the job all right, but these other matters which should be a pleasure produce the utmost anxiety. Some men that I have seen in this position had been hurriedly reading books on art and the literature of the day in a feverish attempt to keep up with the conversation of their contemporaries. Of course the answer is, 'We are what we are, let us be secure in ourselves. Sure. Let us read, but do so for what we get out of it, and not for any superficial social value that it carries with it.'

These men are gifted men, and when they see things in perspective they cope very well; but with their wives it is often different. In general they are both less secure in themselves and more sensitive to the social occasion. I saw one such woman yesterday whom I have helped in this respect by showing her how she can reduce the level of her anxiety through Mental Ataraxis.

Students, whose ability is marginal for the course they are attempting, suffer chronic nervous tension and with it a reduced quality of life. This is an unhappy fact. Many of these students, either from their own desire to work in one of the professions or from pressure from their parents, try desperately hard. Many would be well suited for professional life as the kind of ability which is necessary to pass university examinations is not closely related to the kind of ability which makes for subsequent success in the professions. But I have seen so many students who have developed serious nervous or mental illness in this situation, that I feel very strongly that young people should *not* be led into a course unless they have shown that they have the ability to complete it without too much cost to themselves.

To work with workmates with a cultural background different from ourselves increases our level of anxiety. In these circumstances we feel an outsider. We do not belong. This occurs when an individual of a racial minority comes to work amid members of the indigenous population. In this situation there is often some real discrimination. But even when there is no discrimination and the individual himself is aware that there is no discrimination, the anxiety may still persist. There would seem to be two reasons for this. In the first place it is very difficult for the newcomer to get the feel of the idiomatic and vernacular language of his workmates. This applies particularly to jokes. The newcomer can easily feel that the others are against him when, in fact, they are only joking in all good fun.

I have recently seen a migrant to this country, a French engineer, who said that he was continually ill-at-ease with his workmates because he could not understand their sense of humour.

The other source of anxiety of those from a different culture is more difficult to explain. We all have our roots in the past. Our contact with the past is reassuring to us. This may come about in many different ways, through religion, through social institutions and through family customs. But beyond these obvious associations with the past, there is the empathy generated by the fact that those around us know who we are and whence we came. The individual from the cultural minority lacks this reassurance. Anxiety is higher, and the quality of his life is so much the less.

Work that disrupts our family and personal relationships reduces the quality of our life. This occurs when the partner or parent has to bring back work to do in the evening at home, when he or she is on call or doing shift work at night.

It is also very commonly seen in the young executive who has to make frequent overseas trips. It occurs when our work involves us being moved from place to place, as in service life and work with many large corporations, which may call upon us to serve for periods in different cities or different countries. This state of affairs has become accepted as part of present day existence.

There is often a sense of glamour in these jobs, but this does not compensate for the loss of the more human aspects of living. The wife says to me, 'There is always a move coming up. We can never call the place where we live our home. The children make friends, and then have to leave them and start all over again. It is the same with me.'

We can be compensated for a job that is physically dirty by extra pay, but we cannot be adequately compensated in this way for a job that is morally dirty. There are good salaries ready to entice the unwary. In this respect three areas immediately come to mind. The first concerns work which on the one hand is within the framework of the law, but on the other hand is clearly immoral. Work which involves tax dodging or the circumvention of government regulations comes into this category. If the nature of the work is queried there is always the answer, 'We work strictly within the law. Nobody has anything on us. Anyhow, who are we to question the law?' These glib rationalisations are momentarily reassuring, but they soon lose their power to dispel the disquiet of our mind, and we are faced with a rising discontent within ourselves.

The second category concerns work which involves selling an inferior product. Again management reassures us, 'We can't look after the suckers. If they don't spend their money on this, they will spend it on something else. Anyhow a man must live.' People have consulted me because they have become disturbed in themselves by awareness of the poor quality of the goods which they were required to sell, and others have consulted me because of the unscrupulous selling methods which they were required to use.

The third category consists of people who become aware that the world would be a better place if the whole industry in which they work did not exist. The world would be a better place without their life work. A devastating thought! I have seen people suddenly overwhelmed by it. The rationalisations cease to work. There is no escape; except to something better. It applies to the tobacco industry. It also may affect people whose work in some way involves a war industry, scientists and others working on nuclear projects and those whose work necessitates further pollution of our environment.

In general women attain greater satisfaction in work which gives them scope to use their empathy as well as their reason. This is something quite important. Let us look at it this way. Over the centuries, by the process of evolution various mental reactions which have helped in our survival have become bred into us. Children of a mother who could appreciate how they felt while they were yet too young to tell her in words, had a better chance of survival. It is our empathy which enables us to do this, and women have this capacity to a greater degree than men. By the process of empathy woman has developed the ability to understand how other people feel. These qualities have helped her in mothering, and can also help her in her job. Man, on the other hand, as provider and protector, had greater need of reason and logic.

A woman gains added satisfaction in work in which she can use these qualities to advantage. A good nurse can feel what the patient needs when the patient is unable to express himself. Such qualities are invaluable in medicine and in social work in general. Similarly in architecture, a woman has a better capacity to feel what will make people comfortable than has a man.

A man's way of life at work may become a serious cause of anxiety if it is inconsistent with his wife's expectations. Men who see me as patients often talk about this. Frequently the idea has never been expressed by the wife, but the man is still aware of it. Many times I have said, 'This is what your wife says', and the patient has answered, 'Oh, no, she has never said anything, but I know how she feels'. This situation often occurs when the wife, who has married a successful man of business, comes from a professional family of doctors or lawyers. Somehow the extra money does not make up for various subtle intangibles, real or imaginary, which she feels that she has lost. And the man's way of life at work, however successful, cannot compensate for her feeling of loss.

Of course the situation is often much more blatant than this, and it is simply a matter of an ambitious and discontented woman hounding her less competent husband towards greater financial success or social status.

How does a man deal with such a situation? The wife would say, 'Change your job. Start again', but, of course, a full way of life as a businessman is superior to an inferior way of life in one of the professions. The real answer is something else. The problem really arises only when the man is insecure in himself. If he can attain some inner philosophy he is free of such a problem, and, more importantly, his attitude of mind will gradually influence his wife so that she is no longer restless from these less than ideal values of life.

The most common cause of nervous tension arising through work is not from the work itself but is from the need to control aggressive feelings. The problem is obvious enough. It is extremely widespread and is equally destructive in all strata of society. When we are treated aggressively by the boss, whether he is a lowly foreman or a top executive, the effect is just the same. Our own aggression is aroused, but we cannot give it vent or we shall lose our job. So we control it, bottle it up, inhibit it, and in doing so we become tense. However, when we gain ease of mind we are beyond these primitive reactions. Then it is no longer someone threatening us with his aggression, so that we automatically respond with our own aggression and have to inhibit it. It is, rather, just a fact, a phenomenon, someone 'blowing off' because they cannot cope with a life situation, and we ourselves are unmoved by it.

Our way of life at work must be within our capacity, leaving us some reserve of both physical and mental energy. I have seen many people as patients who have broken down with chronic anxiety through failure to follow this simple rule. In these days of shorter working hours many men have two jobs, or one full time job and one part time. They are lured on by high wages, but have little in reserve, and some additional minor stress, which they would normally be able to ignore, is sufficient to produce psychosomatic symptoms.

At a higher level, there is the business executive who cannot resist taking on yet another board. The successful doctor will not limit the number of patients whom he sees, and adds to the work load by accepting every invitation to lecture. People wonder at their selfless devotion to duty. But, in fact, they are leading a life of inferior quality which is inevitably reflected in the standard of the work that he does.

Then there are women who over-estimate their capacity to do two jobs. They rush home from work to cook the evening meal and attend to the children. They are up early in the morning with household chores. They have nothing in reserve, either mentally or physically, their tension shows in irritability with the children and their own sense of increasing anxiety, and the quality of their life deteriorates.

Should we leave our problems at the office or factory, or should they be taken home with us? Patients have often said to me, 'I wish I did not have to bring home all this work every night.' Others who don't have to bring home work have said, 'I wish I could forget about the office when I go home. But I can't. The worry of it is with me all the time.' This is said, not only by executives, but also by those of quite modest status. There is something wrong here. These people are working with a high level of anxiety that is spoiling the quality of their life. They cope better if they reduce the level of their anxiety with the practice of relaxing meditative experience; but the work situation itself requires re-evaluation. It is probable that they are working too close up to the limit of their capacity.

When our work is biologically significant it becomes part of our whole life. The mother and housewife does not put matters of the family out of her mind at 6 p.m.; nor would she wish to. The farmer comes in at sunset, and in the summer it is a long day; but in the evening it is natural to him to ponder the problems of the season, and he would not want it otherwise. The scientist, the artist or the writer does not try to dismiss the subject of his work from his thoughts. Nor does the teacher, the nurse or the social worker. In fact, when we are engaged in occupations that have some meaning in the biological sense, we rather like to think in relaxed fashion about the work that we do. This means that our work is fulfilling to us. So bringing home work in these circumstances is something quite natural and will not of itself cause anxiety.

However for all those hundreds of thousands of people who do purely repetitive work the situation is quite different. They can best cope with their lives by psychological dissociation whereby they come to lead two lives, one at work and one away from work, and in this way the automated, materialistic part of their life is shut off from the human aspect of their being.

Some people compensate in their leisure hours for their un-balanced way of life at work. Those whose work is routine and repetitive may compensate with intellectual pursuits in their leisure. On the other hand, the executive whose work is intellectually exacting often spends a good deal of his leisure in frivolous activity which may belie his essentially serious disposition and mislead his friends into thinking of him as a playboy. The fact that this type of compensation is necessary indicates that there is something wrong with the work situation. If our work is fulfilling to us we have a great capacity for exacting intellectual activity without need of this type of compensation. It is only when a high level of anxiety is added to exacting intellectual activity that we need to compensate in this way.

Our work must be consistent with our spiritual striving. This is a more difficult proposition to establish, and you may well feel, 'This does not concern me. I have no spiritual striving.'

In more than thirty years as a psychiatrist I have come to know that we are often unaware of much of the spiritual striving that goes on within us. In a way it embarrasses us, so we use the simple psychological defence of denial; and we deny to ourselves that we have these feelings. Yet in psychotherapy they come out in unxspected fashion, especially in young people. With different individuals these feelings become associated with different areas of life, with wife and family, with nature or with God.

Different people relate their spiritual striving to their work in different ways. By strange coincidence, only yesterday morning I saw two patients who demonstrate the point which I wish to make. One was a very religious, idealistic man. His job was secretary to a branch of a political party. His work and his spiritual striving are completely integrated as he believes the world can become a better place through his political work. The other patient was a young bank officer. He also is very religious and there is a marked spiritual aspect to his life. Probably, this aspect of his inner life has been accentuated by a severe organic illness suffered some years ago. He likes his work at the bank, but it is just his job, and it is in no way associated with this other aspect of his life which concerns church activities in the weekends. This process is known as psychological dissociation and it allows us to separate different aspects of our life mentally just as we do physically.

Does our life's work help ourselves and others, either within the family or in the community at large, to be better people? You may well say that I am becoming too idealistic. That I have moved from the practical biological and psychological effects of our work into something else which neither of us understands too well. You may say that you do not know what being a better person really means. I don't understand it very clearly either. But although I do not understand it very clearly, I feel very sure that the general idea of it is valid; that some people do, in fact, help themselves and others to be better people, and that this is often related in some way to their life's work. I am not thinking of religious teachers, peace workers, dedicated doctors, devoted social workers or others in similar fields. I am thinking of something beyond this. It is rather vague and difficult to communicate. I have come to a pause in my writing. The ideas won't clarify. I am strongly tempted to screw up the paper and abandon the attempt to explain what I mean. Let us come back to the original idea. Can our life's work help ourselves and others to be better people? Yes. It can – if we participate in it fully. Take for examples the farmer and the mother. When they are really part of it, their life's work helps them to understand. I am sure that you can go along with me thus far. Well, the next step is simply for us, who live in the great cities and who are neither farmers nor mothers, to learn to extract this element of living from our life's work in a similar way that the farmer and mother so often achieve.

May I make one further comment? There are other valid ways in which our mind can work besides the logical way. The matter which we are discussing is in this other area. I am communicating to you in writing. This is a logical way and is, in fact, quite inappropriate to the matter in hand. If I could see you, if for instance I could personally show you something of the meditative experience beyond relaxation, then in this experience I could clearly communicate the idea which becomes so elusive when I attempt to enslave it in words. But there is one thing that is certain. Mental Ataraxis can in fact bring our mind to a way of functioning in which our work becomes easier and our whole life moves towards greater fulfilment in the Discipline of Ease.

OUR LIFE AT HOME

Life is better when we can look upon our home as a refuge from the stress of the outside world. We come in the door and feel, 'It's good to be home'. Then we know that this part of our life is indeed what it ought to be. In the past, our home or our cave or our hut has been the place where we were safe from the physical discomforts of the weather and danger from our enemies. It was our shelter and we felt safe there; but now the emphasis has changed. We are no longer physically threatened by the weather or enemies. It is now the mental stress of modern, materialistic living that threatens us. Nevertheless, coming home still rekindles within us the psychological response of our forebears and relieves our present anxieties just as it did with the more obvious dangers of the past.

We must not let our home degenerate into a funk-hole from the cross fire of difficult interpersonal relations and the practical problems of our working life. This can happen quite easily with both men and women. It happens mainly with introverts. Those of us who are introverted are likely to become tense in the company of our fellows and in coping with the business affairs of everyday life. By withdrawing from these situations we become more at ease and feel so much the better and there is no easier way of withdrawal than that which leads into a warm and loving home atmosphere. The shy, introverted child does this to avoid the stress of school. A headache or an imaginary attack of 'flu' tempts many an adult to exploit the situation in similar fashion, and we escape from the tensions of work for another day in the security of our home.

The fact of coming home reactivates past emotional experiences. As children, when we first went to school, we found it quite a stressful experience. It was good to get home. Our tensions and anxieties quietened down with mother there and we felt the comfort of familiar surroundings. During our life the circumstances of our home have changed, but coming home reactivates the old psychological reaction which we established in our childhood.

The man who comes home to a secure emotional relationship

with his wife soon feels more secure as regards other matters. Some men, indoctrinated in the mores of the he-man culture of our time, try to deny this. They feel that to be influenced by their wife in this way shows lack of masculine strength and independence. This is a culturally determined reaction. We are what we are. To deny this is only pretence. The mature adult man has a complicated pattern of inter-dependent reactions with his wife just as the child has with his mother. I think there are only two exceptions to this general statement; the psychopath who is unable to develop positive feelings towards his fellows, and the eastern mystic who purposefully practises the philosophy of non-attachment.

The woman who looks forward to her husband's return adds a new dimension to her life. However women have often spoken to me of the mixed feelings with which they await their husband's return. 'I am lonely and I want him back, but I know as soon as he is back we will start bickering. It is an awful life for a woman. I am tired and on edge. Then he comes in. He hardly gives me a kiss. I can see how irritable he is. It makes me feel more edgy than ever. Yet I love him. I would not change him for anyone else.' This less than human experience of life is the lot of many of those around us.

What are the factors which produce the feeling of warmth and security in the home. The answer is simple. One factor exceeds all others in significance. It is love. I have discussed the psychological and spiritual reactions of love elsewhere,* but as regards home making and home life, there is one particularly important aspect. It is the complete psychological identification of the one with the other. Strangely enough, over the last few years I have seen a number of young people who have openly admitted that they were frightened of such a degree of commitment. They have been mainly university students, a number of them studying psychology. They had become conscious of a lack of personal identity, and they felt that a love relationship in which they fully identified with their loved one would further threaten their own sense of inner identity. Of course this is the distorted reasoning of an anxious mind. It is really only through intimate experience with another that we fully attain our own identity.

*MEARES, Ainslie, *Let's Be Human* Fontana, Great Britain, 1976.

The degree to which home gives us a sense of security depends very much on the consistency of reaction of the members. There is a sense of security in a home in which the wife knows how her husband will react, and he knows how she will, and the children are likewise sure of their parents' reactions. If, in each case, the anticipated reaction is one of understanding a real sense of security pervades the whole household. Even when the predicted reaction is one of severity, the individual knows where he stands and unconsciously mobilises psychological defences to deal with the situation. However, if the reactions of the others are unpredictable, the individual remains basically insecure as he is unable to prepare himself psychologically to meet the situation. Of course this reaction is at its maximum intensity when one expects an understanding reponse only to be confronted with one of severity.

What is the authority of the home? Is it autocratic, democratic or mutually cooperative? Of course a home of autocratic authority, whether it be patriarchal or matriarchal, inhibits the freedom of the lesser members. They, in turn, rebel in indirect ways within the home, and seek a compensatory freedom in their own activities outside the home. These reactions are common in our society at the present time, and we see many instances of the compensatory seeking of freedom outside the home extending into violent and anti-social behaviour. Nevertheless, an autocratic home, provided that it is not overdone, can contribute to our well-being in that it tends to reduce our level of anxiety. It is like being in the services. We know where we stand, and the responsibility of decision making is at a minimum.

Problems arise with changes of authority in the home. I saw many examples of this after the war. The husband had been away for three or four years, and the wife had successfully fulfilled the dual role of both mother and father to the children. The return of the father necessitated the re-establishment of natural roles. There were uncertainties, problems, and often conflicts with consequent anxiety and various psychosomatic symptoms in both husband and wife.

I have observed the same process in more subtle form in other circumstances. The husband has been a tense, anxious, insecure man; and the wife has assumed the dominant role in the household. The man's anxiety has gradually increased to the point at which he has sought professional help. As a result of treatment he has gained greater ease of mind and a greater sense of security. His increased capacity for self assertion has brought about a power struggle to regain the dominant role which he had relinquished on account of his nervous condition.

The democratic household does not work as well as one might expect. Or this would appear to be so from my experience in talking with patients. I think a number of factors come into this. The concept of democracy is really an intellectual ideal rather than a part of the process of evolution, so it does not fit too easily into the basic biological situation of the family.

Two other factors have struck me as particularly significant. It has nearly always been the wife who has emphasised to me that she and her husband enjoy a democratic form of home life. The wife has often said something like this, 'I see to it that we always discuss our problems together'. It has become clear to me that in many of these households the emphasis on a democratic form of family life is really only a masquerade for a new form of twentieth century matriarchy. The other factor which I have observed is that in families who have evolved a democratic structure the man is usually rather passive by nature.

The greatest problem in the democratic family is the same as in democracy in general. Younger members of the family come to claim an equal right in making decisions, the results of which they cannot properly assess.

A family which is neither autocratic, nor democratic, but which just goes along intuitively may attain a better way of life. This is something that we can sense rather than argue logically. Perhaps we can understand better if we look at it this way. The autocratic family is the product of our biological heritage. The democratic organisation of family life is an intellectual ideal. On the other hand, the intuitively cooperative family represents a further advance in the evolutionary process. In such a family there are no commands or orders, no family conferences, but things just happen the right way. For such a pattern of life the individuals must be intelligent, sensitive and intuitive. In other words they have progressed further than most of us along the path of human evolution.

Do some members of the family feel the home atmosphere oppressive? We must ask ourselves about this as all of us are not sufficiently empathic to know automatically how the others feel. Many times I have had teenagers and those in their early twenties complain of the oppressive atmosphere of the home. When I have mentioned this to their parents, they have been astounded. They were quite unaware that the others felt this way.

The opposite reaction is also quite common. It is, in fact, much more common than most people would suspect. The behaviour of the teenagers produces an atmosphere which the parents find oppressive. Sometimes this is purposive, either consciously or unconsciously, but the parents are frightened to take appropriate action lest the teenagers suddenly leave home and become exposed to moral hazards with which the parents feel they are not sufficiently mature to cope. In this situation it is the teenagers who hold the authority, and it is the parents who are oppressed by it.

Do the individual members of the household share similar political, religious and sociological attitudes? A generation ago people in the neighbourhood could point to a house and say, 'The people who live there are church-going folk, or they support such and such a political party'. However, now things are different. It is rare for the family to go to church as a whole. It is more often a matter of one or two members going and the others staying away. Similarly with politics. The family no longer votes as a political unity. The children frequently vote differently from their parents, and it is not uncommon for husband and wife to support different political parties.

This has largely come about through the present day emphasis on individual identity. Although it is a neurotic reaction, the man, woman or child who purposefully takes up an attitude different from the rest of the family, feels that he is asserting his own individuality, and feels that he gains strength from what he is doing. The young person needs to break free from his parents to establish his own status as an adult. How better than not going to church when they go, or even going when they never go. Or voting for the other party! This is felt as clear evidence of individual identity and adult stature.

Similar reactions occur in many young women. They tend towards the Women's Liberation Movement; they want to be an individual in their own right and not pale shadows following every movement of their husband. So they go to church, or otherwise, according to their own inclination; and similarly with their voting. This seems reasonable enough. But in these circumstances people tend to over-react. Women have told me that they have voted for the other party from their husband just to demonstrate to themselves their own identity as a woman. These women have not been in an unhappy marriage situation, wanting to vent their hostility to their husband; they are women who simply want to assert their individuality, and who have chosen this rather odd way of giving the idea expression. With many of us, our attitudes on religious, political and sociological matters are coloured by similar neurotic reactions.

When members of the household share differ political, religious and sociological attitudes, what is the effect on family life in general? People say, 'None at all, we are all adult, or nearly so, and we are all entitled to our individual opinions'. The parents say this. But they say it so quickly that I am sure that it is not the whole truth. Often the parents have the vague and disturbing awareness that the young people's vote is determined by idealistic and humanistic reasons as opposed to their own practical and materialistic considerations. With others, there is an equally vague and disturbing awareness that the contrary votes in the home are a strange expression of hostility against themselves.

Many people pride themselves on a closely knit family of free thinking and independently acting members. Patients have often thought that they had achieved this. But discussion with other members of the family has almost always disclosed that the closeness has been a masquerade, a pretending, and a simple denial to the self of the facts of reality. We all do this to greater or lesser degree. We pretend, and we deny things to save ourself the hurt of facing a reality which seems too difficult for us. So it is within the family. These reactions are usually supported by a lack of real communication. The individual feels that if he were to express his differences with the others, it would all be too difficult, and family unity would be disrupted. So the avoidance of real communication becomes a psychological defence, and the illusion of family closeness is preserved.

Do members of the household usually side the same way in controversial questions? For instance, do mother and the children side together against father, or mother and son against father and daughter, or parents against the children? Families whose members develop a constant pattern of allegiance tend to fall into conflict over increasingly trivial matters. On the other hand, if the pattern of allegiance is not firmly fixed, matters of difference in the family circle are more easily resolved.

Are there basic conflicts in the home in which the parents rigidly adhere to establishmentarian ideas and the children have come to hold more modern concepts of morality? There is some element of this conflict in the lives of most of us. In a way it is an inevitable part of progress, but we, the older generation, should be able to listen to new ideas, and to accept some changes in what we have come to regard as appropriate behaviour. But it does not always work out like this. And it often comes about that the two parties of the conflict are so insecure in themselves that they become defensively entrenched in their own ideas so that discussion and compromise become impossible, and the quality of home life is marred by a running battle with continual sniping from both sides.

Does the prevailing atmosphere of the home tend towards the puritanical or towards the hedonistic? When confronted with such a question, we immediately react with the thought, 'My home is neither puritanical nor hedonistic'. This is the opinion we have of ourselves, but if we come to think of the homes of other people whom we know well, we can often see that the atmosphere is tinged in this respect, the one way or the other. The puritanical home is strict and rigid. In the minds of the individuals of the household right is right and wrong is wrong. The two are clearly distinguished, and this distinction is often made on a basis of religious teaching. And when something is wrong it is avoided. On the other hand, in the hedonistic home the general mood is one of freedom and the salient question is, 'How can I enjoy myself'. Smoking, drinking, gambling, flirting and extra-marital sexual experience are really all a part of life, and are to be enjoyed without becoming moral issues. Think of the homes of some of your friends, and I am sure most of them will tend in one direction or the other.

The unexpressed rules of the puritanical home have their effect on all concerned. If the individual accepts the rules as to what is right and wrong, and if he keeps to them, he is freed from the problem of making decisions on moral issues, and consequently enjoys a lower level of anxiety. This is the effect of the puritanical home when it functions at its optimum. But if the individual is unable to accept all the rules of conduct, he becomes filled with uncertainty. He is possessed with guilt and the level of his anxiety is increased so that the quality of his life deteriorates.

The discipline of the puritanical home brings each of its members to exert a very considerable degree of self-control. This is a learning experience of great value which helps the individual to cope better with many of his everyday life situations. This is all to the good; but a problem may arise when the parent indirectly sets too high a standard for the self discipline of the others. He forgets that the self discipline, which he can exert upon himself without too much effort, may in fact be beyond the capacity of other members of the household. He thinks, 'What I can do, they can do. It is only a matter of moral fibre.' But it is not as simple as this. He is older, his personality has matured, and is consequently better integrated. It may be still more complex. People like this whom I have been able to study have often displayed masochistic traits in their personality. They have in fact enjoyed a kind of perverse pleasure in the hardships which their high degree of self discipline has brought upon themselves. This reaction – the perverse feeling of pleasure arising from the discomfort of self discipline – must be clearly distinguished from the normal feeling of satisfaction in being in command of oneself in times of stress, which is the natural reward of the disciplined life.

The puritanical home sets rigid value systems. Right is right, and wrong is wrong. As long as we abide by the rules, a rigid value system assists us in that it helps us to be more sure of ourselves and so reduce the level of our anxiety. But everything is not really clear-cut like this. I can hear the puritan say to me, 'If you have doubts, it is wrong.' But the moral quality of our act is often dependent on the circumstances in which it is committed. Sexual intercourse between loving married partners is universally acclaimed as highly moral, while the same act committed as rape is universally accepted as immoral. There are obviously many circumstances between these two extremes, both within marriage and outside of it, in which the moral quality of the act is less easily defined, and the rigid value system of the puritanical home breaks down.

There is another problem about rigid value systems. Things are never truly black or white. They are always shades of grey. The rigid value system makes questions of right and wrong easier for us, but produces a polarity of thought which does not represent the facts as they really are.

Some aspects of the free living of the hedonistic home add to the quality of our life, while other aspects detract from it. We are free to indulge our spontaneity and self expression. There is freedom to experience joy, and the system permits the free development of our personality. However, this very freedom allows and even encourages the development of tawdry values which debase our personality. In the hedonistic home there is a basic lack of self discipline which allows us to avoid any learning process which may be dull, irksome or unpleasant in itself, but which would lead us on in the future to greater joy and more complete fulfilment.

A home atmosphere which encourages free communication adds to the quality of our life. This is something different from the reactions of the close knit family. The bonds of the close knit family are the emotional ties between the members. These are experienced as a part of family life. The situation is accepted as natural. It is not analysed or discussed. On the other hand, in the home of free discussion these emotional bonds may still be present, but there is a free and natural exchange of ideas which continues at all levels, serious, frivolous, personal and general. I make it a habit of casually enquiring of people who see me professionally if others in the family know of the consultation. In the general enquiry about the patient's mode of life, such questions go unnoticed, but they give a good insight into the degree of communication within the home. I have learned that most people, who live in individually isolated fashion within the family, assume that the same situation obtains in other families. Similarly those who are accustomed to open family discussion take it for granted that others do likewise.

In a closely knit family we gain from the support of the others, but the bonds which hold the family together may also impede individual development. The feeling of the closely knit family is very real. If one of the members is having a tough time, ill health, a broken romance, loss of employment, failure in exams, or an unexpected pregnancy, the others rally around and help. In families in which this is the rule, the help is given without words, and is communicated by what is done. The feeling that the others understand softens the blow, and supports the ill-fated member until the normal psychological processes reassert themselves again.

But family support may be restricting and hinder the member's development as an individual in his own right. When the ties between mother and son are too strong, successful marriage is so much the more difficult. In the closely knit family the young person has little training in individual action and decision making on his own initiative and own responsibility. Because of this lack of experience he is held back not only in marriage but also in the other affairs of life.

Those who claim a sophisticated home atmosphere may endanger the more basic virtues. In discussing this, a woman patient once said to me, 'Oh, we are a sophisticated household. We all discuss our sexual affairs together, and we don't worry too much about who is with us or what we have on in the bathroom.' Good. I am sure that freedom, openness and simplicity add to the quality of our life. But it seemed to me that this woman was making a parade of pseudo-sophistication. I have seen others, both men and women, who have fallen into this type of reaction in less degree. They have been caught up in the glamour of what they regard as the new life so that it becomes a facade, and the more basic qualities of living are ignored.

The sophisticated person explores new ideas of morality and interpersonal relations. This is all to the good. As an animal species we are subject to growth and change, and our social organisation is constantly undergoing modification and development. In order to evolve into a more truly human form of life we must continually explore new ideas. As a result of probing by the more sophisticated among us, our concepts of morality and what is proper in interpersonal relations are continually changing. So long as the motive is the search for something better we gain by this process, but if the search is simply for something different, rather than something better, the new patterns of behaviour are likely to reduce our sense of fulfilment in life rather than increase it. This process is well demonstrated in pseudo-sophisticated families and groups of persons who seek something new in drug-taking, homosexuality and sexual experimentation beyond the expression of love.

The atmosphere of a home in which the members have a traditional occupation affects different members in different ways. This is most clearly seen in the homes of the professional class in which there is a tradition in law, medicine, or the church. It is also seen in the homes of the aristocracy, those on the land and in artisan families. In each there is an unexpressed family consensus of opinion as to what is expected of the individual. The children are expected to carry on the tradition. The father gains purpose in life in the knowledge that what he learns and what he does will be of direct value to the children. In turn the children gain in security. Such a system works well in times of social stability, but in times of social change, such as we are experiencing at present, the system breaks down. The young people are disenchanted with what they see about them, and react against the establishment in general, which includes the traditional organisation of their own particular family group.

We can often sense that the atmosphere of a home is predominantly materialistic or predominantly humanistic. In some homes money, and the cost of things, are frequent subjects of conversation. In others it is hardly mentioned.

The money-mindedness of the home does not depend on economic factors. It is seen in the homes of the wealthy as well as the poor. And many homes in which money is rarely mentioned may still be excessively materialistic in outlook. Sometimes we can gauge this from the motives disclosed by the members. The attitude is that I shall do something for some purpose, and it always turns out to be some purpose of material gain, rather than for love or friendship. If the purpose is one of friendship there is often some ulterior gain in the background. This is a code of practical and realistic living. It has its biological origin in the concept that life is a matter of every man for himself. Those who take practical steps to look after themselves live on, while those who fail to do so are lost in the fight for survival. So also it is in the business world of today.

However, the march of evolution has brought us beyond these primitive reactions. We have learned to think of our fellows and sometimes to consider them even to our own cost. This is something new in the development of man, distinguishing him from the pre-human primitive of the stone age. In some homes we sense a prevailing humanistic orientation. The members are different from those of the materialistic home. In the evolutionary scale they have developed a more fully human pattern of life.

There are two basic tests as to the home atmosphere. Do you and others enjoy returning home? How does the visitor feel in your house? Don't forget that the others may not feel the same way as you do. Parents often assume that the children look forward to returning home in just the same way as they do. This may not be so, and often it is the reverse situation with the children finding a sense of security in the home which their parents do not completely share.

The visitor is often more sensitive to the home atmosphere than are the members themselves. This is so because the members have become accustomed to it and accept their pattern of inter-personal relations as normal. A child visitor may give the parents quite alarming insights. This has come to my notice through talking with parents. The story has been that their child has had a friend to the home. The children have played and talked together, and the child has innocently passed on the visitor's comments to his mother. She has been aghast. 'I did not think we were different from other people.'

Is the atmosphere of the home such that the children can leave it when the time comes that they should? If the ties are too strong, it becomes difficult for the children to leave home and start a life of their own. This applies particularly to the mother-son relationship. But it is sometimes more diffuse, and rather than one strong tie to mother it is a matter of many little threads which combine to make leaving home so difficult. The ideal of course is a combination of closeness with freedom, and when the time comes the individual is free to start his own life.

When the family is moving either upward or downward in social and economic status, there is greater instability and greater anxiety. This is inevitable. In doing new things we are less secure than we were doing the old routine things of life. This essential insecurity increases our anxiety and with it our tendency to psychosomatic symptoms. A surprising number of people who consult me professionally come into this category. Very often the wife is unable to adjust to the new circumstances of life brought about by her husband's success.

I have observed that the successful adult children of working class migrants often bring their parents with them as they move upward, but the parents are unable to adjust to their new status, and become tense and bewildered. Downward movements of a family are often due to the husband having rather less intellectual ability than his father; and of course alcoholism, gambling, mental illness and a broken marriage are common causes of setting a family on the downward path.

Those who live in isolated homes lack leisure time contact with their fellows. This is not only a matter of geographical isolation with people living on isolated farms. I am thinking rather of those families in the great industrial cities who have lost or who have never had the art of becoming part of the neighbourhood in which they live. The causes are many. Families of racial and religious minorities suffer in this way, so do families in which both the mother and father are strongly introverted. Families that are moving downward socially and economically from any cause tend to be avoided by those about them. And of course people who develop unattractive personality traits such as boastfulness, obsequiousness, or suspicion as psychological defences tend to become friendless and isolated.

In our home life we must strike a balance between open sharing and individual privacy. We must remember that our needs in this respect are very different. Extraverts, men and women, boys and girls, need a home atmosphere in which they can openly share their thoughts and feelings with the others. But introverts have a compelling need for some degree of quiet seclusion in which they can let their mind run freely and at the same time examine their own thoughts and feelings. This principle is clearly exemplified in the way that extraverts adjust well to the barrack-room life of the services, while introverts find it so difficult. On the other hand introverts adjust more easily to a secluded academic life. Within the home we must allow individual members freedom to establish the pattern of life which suits their own personality. At the same time we must lead the extravert from too-open sharing and the introvert from excessive seclusion, as excess in either case may distort the personality to the extent of impairing normal adjustments to life situations.

The members of the household must be free to follow their individual interests and hobbies. This would seem obvious enough. But I have spoken to quite a few people who have said something to this effect, 'I would like to do such and such, but the others would not go along with it.' It often refers to some attempt at creativity, particularly painting or pottery, at other times it is a matter of study of some cultural subject. The less sensitive members of the household do not raise any practical objections, but the individual is deterred by their friendly ridicule. 'Fancy Dad as a painter'. 'Mum can bake her pottery with the cakes'. Of course we should not be dissuaded by such light-hearted criticism. But we are sensitive. And those embarking on new interests and hobbies are often very sensitive in these particular areas.

Home life is best when we are flexible in our roles of giving and of accepting dependence. Husband and wife are mutually inter-dependent. We must remember this. An absence of emotional give and take only occurs in the schizophrenic, the psychopath and the eastern mystic practising non-attachment. The wife is dependent on her husband in some areas, and he is dependent on her in others. The point that I am making is that we should guard ourselves against letting these areas of giving and of accepting dependence become too fixed and rigidly defined. We must be able to switch roles according to the needs of the other.

The same principle applies with the adolescent and young adult children. Because of their biological status in life they have grown to accept dependence, but as the wheel of life turns the time will come when the ageing parents need to depend on their children. So we must not become fixed in our inter-dependent roles. If this happens parents in later life find it hard to accept emotional support from their children.

Perhaps even more important is a moment to moment flexibility so that we can mutually support each other in intuitive fashion in all the various traumas, great and small, of everyday living. This kind of flexibility comes to us through Mental Ataraxis. There is ease about us and our ease influences other members of the household, and we move towards greater fulfilment as the Discipline of Ease becomes a part of our everyday life.

I I

OUR SEX LIFE

'Do you enjoy your sex life together?' This is the usual question of the psychiatrist. But we must go further than this. 'Does your sex life add to the quality of your life or does it detract from it?'

I often put the question, 'Do you enjoy your sex life?' only to receive the answer, 'She does not complain.' Other men have unhesitatingly said that they do enjoy it, but when they have come to talk freely, they have disclosed that it is often a one-sided affair. If this is the case, it detracts from the quality of their life rather than adding to it. It is the same with women. Some say, 'I never refuse. I think men need it.' Others, 'Sure, I enjoy the release it gives me.' But with others, particularly young men and women, it has often been quite different. They describe the act of experiencing each other in sex in terms that are nothing less than poetic. They are uplifted by it, and the experience has a profound effect in moulding their emotional reactions, not only the one with the other, but extending into the ordinary affairs of their daily life. I know this to be so as I have had a professional knowledge of some young people, both girls and young men, for some time prior to marriage or cohabitation and for some time afterwards. It has become clear that some have enhanced the quality of their life through sexual experience in a way beyond the normal maturation and confidence which accompanies marriage particularly in young people of introvert personality.

Some couples are able to use their sex relationships to enhance and enrich their emotional life over many years of marriage. As a result they gain something in the quality of their life. From talking with such people I have learned that many factors contribute to the end result. With different couples different factors are important to varying degree. Many of these factors are not consciously contrived by the persons concerned but result from intuitive responses of which the individual is scarcely aware.

Giving and receiving in sex enhances the capacity of our mind for giving and receiving in other areas of life. I am talking of something very much more than the man giving his sperm and the woman receiving it. There is a giving and receiving of the emotions. More – of the very self. And it is a giving and receiving, with both parties as givers and both as receivers. In this there is absolute giving. Everything. Utter and without stint. And at the same time absolute receiving. Absolute, and without qualms or greed.

Much of our interaction with our fellows concerns material giving and receiving. Many of us find it hard to give freely, and in a strange way we are equally ill at ease in receiving openly. But our giving and receiving extends far beyond our material interactions with our fellows. It is the very core of our emotional life. We give friendship and we receive friendship. We give love and likewise receive it. So it is with tenderness and all the gamut of emotions which go to make our experience of human life. In the giving and receiving of sex we enhance our capacity for fully human experience.

In sex we can add a new dimension to our human existence through the experience of defencelessness. In full sexual intimacy there is absolutely no guardedness whatsoever. There is complete abandonment in this absence of guardedness. This is a state of mind seldom experienced in full consciousness. It occurs in the unconsciousness of sleep and in the disturbed consciousness of some states of ecstasy and also in Mental Ataraxis. But in sex we experience defencelessness in the intimate presence of another. In these other conditions, if we are touched, we usually come out of our defenceless state. We are alert again, and our defences are mobilised. But in sex we go with the touch or even the hurt, and the defencelessness is allowed to continue. Again, if we are questioned when asleep or in an ecstatic state, we become alerted and our normal psychological defensive mechanisms become active again; but in sex, the defencelessness continues, and ideas of any nature, even ideas that might be harmful to ourselves, pour from our lips unchecked.

What is the significance of the experience of defencelessness in sex as regards the quality of life? It is this. Most of our habitual attitudes of mind, our aggressiveness, our suspicion, our timidity, our self assertion and all the other various attitudes of mind are, in fact, protective stances. The defencelessness of full sexual intimacy can become a learning experience which leads us towards greater openness of character.

There are three essentials which need to be present for these uplifting effects of sexual experience to come about. These are love, a sensitivity to the other's needs, and an absence of anxiety. When these conditions are present the uplifting effect takes place spontaneously, without contriving, and without the full awareness of the individuals concerned. It just happens this way.

Sexual experience which enhances the quality of our life must be based on love otherwise these favourable psychological reactions do not occur. But the process involves a two way reaction. Love is necessary for sex to be an uplifting experience, as without love the defencelessness, which allows these other reactions, is impossible. On the other hand the physical union facilitates the more complete psychological identification and introjection and so still further enriches the experience of love.

We must be sensitive to our partner's needs. If we are in love we are automatically sensitive to our partner's needs because his wishes become our wishes and his ideas become our ideas. This comes about through the processes of identification and intro- jection and not in response to any logical activity of the mind, but these processes operate in varying degrees of completeness. Many young couples feel that they are in love, but the ultimate experience in identification and introjection has not occurred, and their sensitivity to the other's needs has not reached the pitch that would enable them to lead each other into the com- plete union of utter defencelessness.

Anxiety inhibits full sexual experience. It is this that deprives so many men and women, both young and old, of the full life. If we are tense and anxious we cannot let go. In most of the affairs of ordinary life we cover up our nervous tension, and we get by without too much discomfort. But this approach will not do for sex. Our sex must be genuine and real with no cover up at all. In this respect I would emphasise to you that many men and women, who have suffered in this way, have been able to reduce their anxiety through Mental Ataraxis. As a result the quality of their sexual experience has been enhanced both physiologically and psychologically in a way that they had not thought possible.

Earlier this week I saw a woman who has been consulting me for some months on account of chronic anxiety. She told me that sex had always been a problem to her because of her frigidity. But since she had reduced the level of her nervous tension through relaxing meditative experience, her sex life had quite changed. She is now free to experience multiple orgasms. This change has come about purely as a result of her meditative experience and without any discussion of sexual matters whatsoever. She emphasised that it was not only her sex life which had so dramatically improved but also her whole experience of living.

Variety in sexual experience is part of our general attitude of keeping our mind free to do new things. 'It was so good last time, let us have it the same way again tonight.' Good. And perhaps next time too. And even the time after. But for always. No. Like so many other things, we can get bogged down in routines. Spontaneity is lost. What was an adventure becomes ordinary. New approaches to the body unfold new aspects of the mind, and both partners grow in the experience.

The experience of tenderness in sex helps us to establish tender reactions in other areas of life. I would like to distinguish between two types of tender reactions. On the one hand, there are very active instinctive mothering reactions which lead women to tender behaviour, and there are corresponding, but less clearly defined, protective paternal reactions in men. We see this in most species of the higher animals where the mother suckles her young, cares for them and protects them; and, of course, the human mother makes similar instinctive responses. On the other hand, we have learned to extend our tender reactions beyond the instinctive level of caring for the young. Tenderness in this wider concept is an attribute of the human being and a manifestation of an enhanced quality of life. It is further distinguished from the simple instinctive tender reaction of mothering in that it extends beyond the immediate biological needs of tenderness. It also involves the individual in awareness of his reaction and its consequences, whereas instinctive mothering tenderness is basically automatic.

Now, let us apply these ideas to human sexual relationships. There is both giving and receiving of tenderness in a very basic form. This experience is enhanced by the defencelessness of both partners. The giving of tenderness to someone who is defenceless has a profound effect on the giver because there can be no demand for tenderness in such a situation. Similarly the defenceless individual is profoundly affected by being accorded tenderness because he is aware that his partner is not in any way forced to act tenderly. In this way we learn reactions through our sexual experience which come to extend into other areas of our life, and which lead us to a more fully human existence without our being aware of their origin.

The physical unity of sex facilitates the identification and introjection on which love is based. In love we identify with the one whom we love. This means that we place ourself in the other's shoes, as it were. In this way lovers understand the feelings and actions of the loved one. But love goes further than this, and identification progresses to introjection so that the feelings and ideas of the loved one are taken into ourself and are experienced as our own feelings and ideas. In this way a true unity of mind is established. This is manifested in the way that young lovers so commonly voice identical ideas. In sex there is a penetration and a taking in of the one by the other. There is a physical unity. And the sense of bodily identification of the one with the other facilitates and intensifies a similar process in the mind.

The closeness and physical contact in sexual intercourse establishes a new dimension in human communication. Not long ago I was talking with a quietly spoken, serious minded student. 'How can you know a girl until you have had sex with her?' He was not a Don Juan, provoked to sexual conquest to compensate for feelings of his own inadequacy. He was quietly stating a fact of life. We must very carefully distinguish between two different reactions. On the one hand, closeness and physical contact is a part of erotic experience. On the other hand, closeness and physical contact can be simply matters of communication. In a full sexual experience both reactions occur at the same time.

Non-erotic closeness and touch can be used as a means of communicating ideas which by their nature are not readily communicable by words. This is what the student meant when he asked, 'How can you know a girl until you have had sex with her?' This is sex for communication. If we examine things carefully, we soon see that the same process, sex as a means of communication, operates in successful marriage. Let us take a very simple example. If the partners have a difference, it may be of such a nature, or occur in such circumstances that purely verbal reconciliation becomes very difficult. Or it may be that pride, inhibition or other unconscious psychological defences prevent the individual from making a verbal approach to reconciliation. Yet the communication is achieved in intercourse, completely and naturally. In these circumstances sex is primarily a communication and the erotic experience becomes the secondary consideration. As a result of the communication the quality of life of the individual partners is restored.

Sexual experience can bring a new sense of personal identity to the individual. I am not referring to the sense of biological maturity which comes to the individual when a sex life is first established. This is a psychological reaction to a physiological act and occurs independently of whether the experience is uplifting or degrading. Nor am I referring to the sense of initiation. This is a psychological reaction giving the individual the feeling, 'Now I have done what they do. I know how it feels. I am one of them.' Again this reaction occurs irrespective of whether the sexual experience was uplifting or otherwise. In this context it is merely an act which allows the individual to join the elect group, as it were. Instead of this I am referring to the way that sexual experience in favourable circumstances has quite a profound effect on the individual's sense of inner identity. This, in itself, is an uplifting experience. Our sense of individuality is something very precious. We are ourself. Unique. Within the limits of our biological heritage and our early conditioning we are masters of our destiny. This is all part of our inner identity.

There are many of us who are frightened that we might lose something of our precious individuality if we allow a too close relationship with someone else; so we mentally withhold ourselves in sexual experience for fear of being swamped or immersed in the personality of the other. However those who abandon themselves completely gain a new and enhanced sense of inner identity. The fact of having willingly abandoned ourself, of having freely immersed ourself in the other, gives a shape and clarity to our own identity which we cannot otherwise attain.

In sex the awareness of qualities in our partner evokes the experience of similar or reciprocal qualities in ourself which have hitherto remained dormant. The defencelessness of sexual experience allows us awareness of qualities in our partner which in ordinary circumstances remain concealed as a part of our normal psychological protective mechanism. The experience of tenderness in our partner calls forth our own capacity to feel tenderness. The experience of our partner freely giving evokes our own reciprocal reaction of freely accepting. As a result of such experience we ourselves are enriched, and the quality of our life is enhanced.

In sex we can experience depths and heights of our own personality which are otherwise inaccessible to us. Let me explain by a simple example. A person who is chronically tense and anxious continually holds himself in check. He feels that if he were to let go, something terrible would happen to him mentally. There are many such people among us. Calm or ease of mind is an experience which they simply do not know. Such a person, man or woman, may be able to find in the self-abandonment of the sexual relationship previously unknown aspects of his own mind.

In courting we become familiar with the subtlety of each other's emotional responses. This is an exploration of the mind. In sex we explore the body and in doing so come to understand the depths and heights of the mind which we could not otherwise reach. We explore the anatomy and we participate in our partner's physiological responses. It is good, and it is natural. We enjoy it, and it fulfils our need. But at the same time we go far beyond these anatomical and physiological activities. They are simply the means of approach to something deeper and something higher. We share something of the mind which is behind the anatomical and physiological. More than sharing. These anatomical and physiological responses are the stepping stones of the unique path to the innermost places of the other's mind. The path is open as the willing defencelessness of our partner allows free entry. And in the secret places of the other's mind we find things of our own which we did not know we had.

In these matters it is well to remember the basic philosophy which we are considering. The Discipline of Ease comes to us through our Mental Ataraxis. If now we are exposed to some particularly debasing experience, it no longer has the same effect upon us. We understand, we are secure, and the experience does not affect us the same way. On the other hand, when we are exposed to an uplifting experience, we are equally secure; we are open, and we are free in ourselves to benefit by the experience as it comes to us.

12

OUR LEISURE LIFE

We need leisure. Without adequate leisure we come to a stage at which we are unable to carry on effectively. In our racial development we have become accustomed to periods of leisure. There has been the great activity of the hunt followed by rest and leisure after the kill. Likewise rest and leisure followed our tribal fights. In the agrarian phase of our development we worked hard at the sowing, and when the seed was in we had a period of relative idleness followed by the intense activity of the harvest which in turn gave way to further leisure. So it seems that we have inherited a need to alternate periods of activity with periods of leisure rather than to continue on with our life at an even tempo.

Insufficient leisure leads to an increase of nervous tension with the likelihood of psychosomatic discomfort or illness. Too much leisure can also be destructive. In the past this has been a hazard in the life of the rich and well-to-do, but with the advent of the affluent society the basic needs of material existence are readily available to most of us and we are left with the opportunity for greatly increased leisure if we should so desire it. This, of course, can add enormously to the quality of our life; but there is one proviso. We must be able to use our increased leisure time in ways which will ultimately add to our well-being. These include the restorative power of physical rest, the reduction of anxiety, activities which help mature our personality and the inner gains from cultural and creative experience.

Animal-like, we are aware of the restorative effect of physical rest. In a vague way we sense that doing less reduces our feeling of nervous tension; but beyond this most of us have no real knowledge as to how we can best use our leisure. The result is quite predictable. Many spend their increased leisure time in response to the simple hedonistic principle of doing what seems to give immediate pleasure. Drinking, parties, idle prattle, spectator sports, staring uncritically at television, escapist films of violence and pornography, endless reading of the sports news and studying sporting lotteries, meaningless sexual encounters and in the young a tendency to while away the time in the half daze of pot smoking.

It seems a long list of decadent activities. You, the reader, may well say, 'But these or similar pastimes have been the lot of mankind through the ages.' 'Quite so.' But the time has come when we can do better. And the first step in doing better is for us to learn to use our leisure in a way that gives pleasure, gives satisfaction and at the same time enhances the quality of our life. This is a matter of education, and it must start in the schools. We must present the idea to young people in such a fashion that they realise that leisure spent in this greater way is, in fact, enjoyable.

The better we are adjusted psychologically, the less is our need of leisure to maintain health. The tense, anxious neurotic person needs frequent holidays, while the mature, stable although equally active individual continues along without such a compelling need for leisure. True, this person likes his holidays, but if they are postponed for business or family reasons, he does not go to pieces in the same way that his neurotic counterpart does.

The tempo of modern city life does not vary to the same degree as did the tempo of life for the primitive. Now, instead of our phases of inactivity being the natural consequence of our way of life, they are arbitrarily arranged as times of rest in the weekends and our annual holidays. Most of us find these leisure periods necessary for our health. On the other hand there are those people, who are mature in themselves and who are well adjusted psychologically, who are able to continue to work for long periods with little leisure and without impairment of their health. These people have made another step forward in evolutionary development from the need of recurrent phases of leisure which we have inherited from our primitive ancestors.

Our need for leisure becomes less compelling as we ourselves achieve a unity with our lifestyle. Such people are able to work long hours with little leisure and practically no holidays. These are the people who have captured something of the secret of living. They enjoy leisure when it comes to them, and they enjoy their holidays, but there is no compulsive need for either. They are free in themselves. People like this are not confined to any one occupation, but the majority whom I have seen have been farmers. Others have been self-employed artisan types, an occasional doctor, a nurse or two and a few housewives. These people have enjoyed their work without over fatigue, and in the virtual absence of leisure or holidays. These occupations are satisfying in their biological, humanistic and creative aspects, but from my knowledge of these individuals, I do not believe that their happy adjustment to life is due simply to their occupation. It would seem that there has been some kind of interaction of the individual's personality with his occupation, something more than identifying himself with his work, a real integration whereby the man, his job and his life are all the same thing, and, at a deep level of his consciousness, he is aware of this unity.

Some of us have a psychological maladjustment which prevents us from enjoying our leisure. 'Is it right just having an easy time enjoying myself like this? Shouldn't I be getting on with some of my work?' This is the recurrent thought. The student may feel it when he takes a night off from his studies. The over-worked housewife may have the same thought if she sits down to rest for a moment. So also the doctor, lawyer or businessman may spoil his well earned leisure by thoughts that perhaps he really should be reading over some technical journal that he has in his briefcase. People who react in this way usually have well developed obsessive elements in their personality. They unconsciously try to ward off anxiety by attempting to have everything just right. They feel that if they can conscientiously get everything just right there can be nothing to worry about. The idea of leisure conflicts with this tendency to be over-conscientious, and the resultant anxiety makes the individual uncomfortable in himself so that he feels that he would really prefer to be getting on with his work.

People with different types of personality have quite different leisure requirements. This is a matter of some importance. With shorter working hours we have more time for leisure. Governments aware of this are trying to make better provision for people to utilise and enjoy their leisure. In general, those who govern the country, and this goes for all countries, are competent extraverts. If they did not have these qualities they would not be where they are. The problem is that they tend to provide leisure facilities for others which they themselves would enjoy. However, these are not always suitable for others with a different type of personality.

The extravert needs the opportunity for gregarious leisure activity. His general orientation to life is towards the outer reality of things and people, rather than the inner reality of the mind, and his main way of dealing with anxiety is by increasing his sense of security by being with his friends. 'I get a bit uptight at work. Then I have a few drinks with the boys. Seeing them gets me relaxed again.' The extravert gets his relaxation from the company of his friends just as much as from the alcohol. In fact, for him drinking is really just a socially acceptable way of meeting one's friends. On the other hand, the introvert who drinks in similar circumstances obtains relaxation primarily from the alcohol as in the company of others he tends to be tense rather than relaxed. So the extravert, in order to relax, needs leisure activity in the company of others – team games, watching sport with friends and parties of all description. This is what he needs to help him unwind. But there is the other side of the coin. Besides using our leisure for relaxation we can use it in such a way as to further develop ourselves as individuals. I can sense the reader responding, 'But leisure is for fun, not for improving ourselves.' But the two ideas need not clash. We can enjoy what we do, in fact have fun, and at the same time we can be doing something which adds to our stature as a human being. It is a matter of using our leisure in a way that helps develop our personality into something better, something more mature.

The gregarious activity which the extravert enjoys, and which helps him relax does nothing for him in this respect. To aid the further development of his personality the extravert should spend some of his leisure in relaxing thoughtful activity, reading, thinking, just being at ease. In general the extravert does not take too readily to such a quiet and thoughtful way of spending his leisure time. But a little of this interspersed with his parties helps to develop his personality by giving him greater awareness of the inner realities of life. I am sure the reader will have observed this reaction in some extravert friend who has suffered a serious illness, and, as a result, has been cut off from his accustomed gregarious activity and has developed the habit of reading and inner contemplation in a way that has led him into greater maturity as a person.

The introvert enjoys a degree of solitary activity in his leisure. The introvert tends to be concerned with the inner reality of his own mind rather than the outer reality of things and people, and in general his main way of coping with anxiety is by withdrawal. He can unwind by spending his leisure in a quiet time by himself. He does not like team games, but prefers solitary sports such as golf, skiing, sailing, climbing, bushwalking. He also likes reading and solitary hobbies – philately, photography and collecting – and he may spend a lot of time on music or art. The physical and psychological withdrawal associated with these activities help reduce his anxiety. But these activities do not help his personality. For this he needs to mix his solitary leisure pastimes with some more gregarious activity. This helps to mature his personality and brings him greater ease of interpersonal relations. A good friend can be a great help in initiating this process. The young introvert, girl or young man, withdraws from social gatherings to avoid anxiety, but the presence of a friend allays nervous tension and the introvert learns to cope with these situations, and the freer contact with his fellows helps to add a new dimension to his personality.

Obsessives, who tend to be perfectionistic and rigid by nature, enjoy spending their leisure in orderly and well regulated fashion. These people try to manage their anxiety by having everything just right. They feel that if everything is in order there can be nothing to worry about. So they like to spend their leisure in an orderly way making a special time to do this and a special time to do that. Then everything is in order even in leisure times, and anxiety is reduced. They like working in the garden, and their satisfaction comes from having it neat and tidy. If the obsessive is interested in carpentry, he prides himself in the high quality of his work, and you can be sure that all his tools are well kept and each is put away in its proper place. If he goes for a holiday, he likes some definite plan, and he arranges a programme for sightseeing or sporting activity, whatever the case may be. This all fits in with his basic psychological need to have everything orderly so as to reduce his anxiety. It would seem easy enough to depart from this principle. But not for the obsessive. I have seen a number of such people, many of them businessmen, who have become tense, and who have felt that nothing could be better than to laze away the time and relax in summer sunshine on the beach. But they did not know themselves. Each returned more tense and anxious than when he started his holiday. All because the freedom and lack of routine had conflicted with his habitual lifestyle. The obsessive enjoys his leisure most when he spends it in planned and orderly fashion. But this need to be orderly and rigid is constricting to his personality. It makes him too occupied with details so that the broader vista of the outlook evades him. His personality is improved by mixing his orderly leisure pastimes with something that gives him greater freedom. He needs a little experience in abandoning himself, a greater freedom in what he does, a greater freedom in his way of thinking, a greater freedom of emotional experience, in letting his hair down, as it were. If he can achieve moments of this in his leisure, he comes to be less rigid in his ordinary life.

The insecure person, above all else, likes to be safe in his leisure, because his habitual way of avoiding anxiety is in trying to be safe. He takes no risks, either physically, ethically or morally. In its extreme form this reaction results in leisure being spent in a quiet time at home. 'I just like pottering about having an easy time.' Of course, the introvert also tends to stay at home, but this is part of his withdrawal from his fellows, whereas the insecure person stays at home to avoid the dangers of the outside world. Even at home he is careful. No risks at all. Not even the risk of reading modern writers for fear that it might upset him by threatening some of his cherished ideas. So the insecure person comes to lead a constricted life, just as does the obsessive, but for a different reason. Any holiday is necessarily unadventurous, not only as regards any possible physical danger, but also the dangers of coming into contact with undesirable or more robust companions. Sometimes such people, aware of their inherent insecurity and conscious that others may despise them for it, react by over-compensating in their leisure activity. At different times I have seen three very insecure young men as patients who had taken up flying and who had gained their pilot's licence just to show other people that they are really brave and adventurous and not cowardly or insecure at all. Incidentally none of them enjoyed the flying. It was just something that they had to do. This reaction is rather like that of young men who are sexually insecure and in consequence are driven to seduce one girl after the other in an attempt to alleviate their feeling of insecurity. In general, the insecure person is helped by using his leisure in rather more adventurous fashion. I have known a number of very insecure young people, both girls and young men, who have greatly benefited by an overseas trip.

Thus we see that leisure means different things to different people and that the different personalities that make up society must be catered for by a society bent upon extending its leisure time.

Likewise people who understand their own personalities are better able to make use of their leisure time and also to avoid following their inclinations to extremes or in ways that retard personal development.

People whose everyday work involves the care and responsibility of others dependent upon them need to take their leisure away from this situation if possible. A mother needs the opportunity for some leisure activity away from her children. This need varies with different women according to their personality and the demands of the children. I have recently seen a woman with a mentally retarded child of seven, who for practical purposes had never been away from the child. Where mother went the child had to come too. Kindergarten services help most mothers to get some break from the demands of their children. I think that women's need in this respect is becoming greater as their horizons become wider and their aspirations beyond the home become more compelling.

A certain amount of leisure spent in idleness is not time wasted, especially if it leads to repose. We may experience restless idleness, calm idleness or simply drowsy idleness. In each case the condition of our mind is very different, and it has a very different effect on our state of well-being. In restless idleness the level of our anxiety is increased, and both our sense of well-being and our actual well-being are reduced. In drowsy idleness there is a marginal and short-lasting reduction of anxiety. But if we can let the idleness of our leisure moments drift into repose we gain an effective reduction of anxiety and with it greater clarity of thought and freedom of emotional response.

Repose is more than inactivity. In it our mind runs on without restraint and without our full awareness, and in this process greater understanding oftens comes to us. The reduction in the level of our anxiety allows our mind to run in unguarded fashion. It is no longer constrained to be careful and realistic. In this state it is not held back by the practicality of immediate details. It can roam freely in a way that is impossible in the full alertness of our everyday life. Because we are not held back by practical details we get glimpses of the big picture. We see our own problem in relation to a much wider and deeper background. New perspectives of our own situation come to us. More than this. It is in repose, in the apparent idleness of leisure, that a greater understanding of life itself comes to us.

Escapist leisure activity may help us by reducing the level of our anxiety, but it does little else to enhance the quality of our life. In escapist activity our mind is diverted from the problems which are worrying us. In this way it is a defence. The tense businessman has to read a thriller for half an hour before he can get to sleep. It would be much better if he were to reduce his tension by the more natural means of letting his mind experience a few moments of mental relaxation, and then sleep would come naturally to him.

The same activity may be escapist or otherwise according to our state of mind at the time. When we go to visit some friends just because we feel that we must go out, we are engaging in escapist activity in order to divert our minds from the restlessness which we would experience if we remained at home. On the other hand, if we visit the same friends primarily to enjoy their company and fellowship, we are really satisfying the legitimate gregarious needs of our personality. Similarly we may temporarily escape from our problems in drinking, but we can also drink to enjoy the company of our friends or simply to enjoy our natural sense of taste. A bawdy play or film may be an escape, but it can also be a natural means of indulging our sense of humour.

A too-constant and too-intense analysis of the reasons why we do things inhibits our spontaneity and spoils the joy of life. On the other hand we need to keep some watch over our motivation lest we fall into the pattern of excessive escapist activity. If, with a little self examination, we should find that we are given to escapist activity, of course we should mend our ways. In doing this, we find the better path more easily if we first set about reducing the anxiety which has been goading us into escapist pitfalls.

Leisure spent in social activity satisfies our gregarious needs and also our sexual need in sublimated form. In our early days we learned that it was much safer for us if we stayed with our fellows rather than wandered off by ourselves. In this way through the evolutionary process we became gregarious. So our present-day leisure needs to satisfy our human needs in this respect. Social contact with those of the other sex is also important. Sometimes a man and a woman can talk together in circumstances in which their sexuality would seem to be completely repessed and ignored. It is just a matter of contact of one human being with another. But in most of our relationships between man and woman, we are clearly aware that the other person is not our own sex, and we interact the one with the other, on this basis. This awareness of the sexuality of social intercourse activates feelings in both parties. It may be no more than a vague awareness of one's own sex. Leisure contacts of this nature are of value to us. We are reminded of what we are, that we are sexual beings, with sexual roles and sexual appetites.

In playing sport we experience the effects of several different psychological reactions. The game is a contest. At bottom it is a fight between the players. Football, tennis, chess, cards – the contest and the fight is there. It reactivates the feeling of contest which still lurks within us as a heritage from the days when we had to fight to survive. But we also play sports in which the element of contest is not so obvious. Mountaineering, bush-walking, sailing, skiing. These sports reactivate feelings which we experienced as primitives in our great contest with the forces of nature. And, of course, the widespread satisfaction which people experience in gardening owes its joy to the same psychological reaction.

In sport we dissipate our aggression. We have the in-built protective reaction within us to respond to the aggression of others by becoming aggressive ourselves. If the boss at work is directly or indirectly aggressive, or if there are similar problems at home, our aggression is aroused. We have learned the trick of displacing our aggression. Thus aggression aroused by the boss at work may become vented on the wife at home. On the other hand it may be vented in sporting activity, and the general pattern of our life is so much the better. If you, the reader, should find that you are relying on this method, please remember that nervous tension precipitates our aggression. So reduce your nervous tension through the relaxing meditative experience of Mental Ataraxis. Then you will be able to have all the fun and enjoyment of your sport as a symbolic contest without the need of it to dissipate your aggression.

Sport has another important effect on us in that the expression of our aggression is associated with appropriate bodily activity. In primitive times aggression would lead to physical combat. Now we have learned to blow off our aggression in words or by fighting our antagonist indirectly in business or in social oneupmanship. But in sport the process is more direct and much more effective as it is associated with bodily activity just as it was in our primitive times.

In all games there are rules. Keeping to the rules involves the exercise of self-discipline. This is a learning process which helps us in life in general. This is something quite important. In general we come to learn self-discipline through the experience of external discipline enforced upon us through our parents, through our school, through the church and through the law. At our present stage of social evolution these institutions, the family, the school, the church and the law are conspicuously failing in the help that we should get from them in learning and maintaining self-discipline. In these circumstances the self-discipline that we learn in games becomes so much the more important. We see it with toddlers who invent their games and make up their own rules. Each is expected to keep to the rules of the game just as adults are in their more formalised sports.

Games teach us to be good losers as well as good winners. In the game of life we have our failures and our successes. We are likely to react to failure with depression and paranoid attitudes. As with all our emotions there is biological purpose in depression. When we fail or lose the fight, psychological depression helps us to adjust to the inferior status which has come to us. In primitive times it helped us accept the mastery of our vanquisher. However, in modern life this reaction has largely outgrown its usefulness. We are better if we are not too depressed, as we can then take steps to re-establish ourselves. Games teach us to do this. There is no place among sportsmen for the individual who is unduly depressed at defeat.

Another psychological response to failure is the development of a paranoid reaction. This really amounts to blaming something else rather than ourselves. A man fails in business and blames his competitors for being ruthless or acting outside the law. The student fails his exams and blames the system. A marriage breaks up and both parties blame the other. This type of reaction has its biological purpose in saving us the hurt of knowing our own weakness. Of course, it is a much better reaction if the individual is mature enough to accept personal responsibility for his failure. We learn this in our games. 'You were too good for me today.'

Games also help us to adjust to success. Elation, which is the opposite to depression, is the biological reaction to success. When we are elated we are very confident and sure of ourselves. In primitive times this has helped us to take command and exploit the success which we have had. But things have changed, and elation as a result of success now angers other people and turns them against us. In our games we learn to accept our success with modesty, and we gain from this pattern of behaviour in our everyday life.

Spectator sports can also help us. In this the effective psychological mechanism is identification. We identify with our team and the players. Through this identification we can dissipate our own aggression; but the spectator gains much less than the player.

He does not experience the self-discipline of keeping to the rules, nor does he learn from success and failure to the same degree as the players. In fact paranoid reactions, such as blaming the umpire, are more common among the ardent supporters than the players themselves.

There is no doubt that spectator sports are a help to the aged, the infirm and others who may not be able to participate. But there is danger, particularly among young people, in becoming spectators rather than players. We gain in our own initiative and self-reliance in playing a game. The spectator learns nothing of this. It is easy to translate this attitude into life itself, so that we become critics of those who participate actively and critics of the umpiring government, rather than playing the game ourselves.

In an indirect way, hobbies associated with collecting satisfy our primitive acquisitive instinct. In times past, when the struggle for life was more pressing than it is now, those of us who got into the habit of hoarding things, especially food, had a better chance of survival. We have inherited this tendency to hoard and collect. Different people among us show this tendency in quite different ways. There is the housewife who likes to keep her larder and storeroom full even though the ready availability of food makes this quite unnecessary. She just likes it this way because it is a part of her inherited pattern of reaction. If you ask her about it, of course, she rationalises, and says it is well to be prepared for some national disaster. The same psychological mechanism is at work in men who hoard useless odds and ends, and rationalise with the explanation, 'It might just come in handy sometime.' The collector is able to sublimate this primitive urge into something more sophisticated and more satisfying.

In primitive times we envied and respected those who had hoarded things as they were more secure than others. Now we still experience the same reaction in slightly modified form. It is 'in' to be a collector. It gives the individual prestige in the eyes of his fellows even though the things which he collects may be neither useful nor beautiful; but he still enjoys this strange prestige which is the 'flow on' from times past.

Many engage in hobbies simply to divert the mind from pressing problems of everyday life. The hobby takes their mind off the other thing which they would sooner forget for a while. This type of reaction has its value for people who have not acquired the ability of repose. They cannot just sit and rest and let their mind be easy. To get away from their worry they have to occupy their mind actively with something else. And people who believe that they cannot quieten their minds by other means do in fact gain something by using their hobby simply as a means of distraction.

Our hobby needs to fit in with our own individual type of personality. I have known several people who have taken up a hobby simply because a close friend had gained much satisfaction in it. However, the friend was a different personality, and the hobby that suited him so well only brought frustration and irritation to the other person. In general, introvert people gain satisfaction when they work at their hobbies in isolation. Extraverts like hobbies that bring them into contact with plenty of people, and obsessive, perfectionistic people like hobbies that involve thoroughness and orderliness.

On the other hand introverts are benefited by hobbies which bring them into contact with others, extraverts are benefited by hobbies involving some degree of introspection and obsessives by hobbies leading to greater freedom of thought and action. We can see that what the individual likes, and what benefits him, is not always the same. The guiding principle is that our hobby must not be too inconsistent with our personality or it will produce anxiety and the beneficial effect will be lost.

Many hobbies have an elitist aspect which bolsters up our ego. Of course it is only the very insecure among us that need this kind of support. I recollect a lunchtime conversation of a few days ago. The subject was trout fishing. Three of those present were experienced trout fishermen. This gave them superiority and confidence in contrast to the other two at the table; but these others were soon able to switch the topic to skiing at which they are expert and the trout fishermen quite inexperienced. With the change of topic the skiers' egos expanded and those of the trout fishermen contracted. This may all seem rather trivial to the reader, but it illustrates the elitist reaction which may become a part of any hobby.

Creative hobbies satisfy our need to explore new things both materially and in our own inner experience. We all have the urge, in greater or lesser degree, to be creative, to make new things, to test out new ways of doing things, and to explore new patterns of thought and reaction. It was through his creative urge that stone age man established his mastery over other animal species and became able to protect himself from the vicissitudes of nature. All these traits of character, which are of biological advantage to us, such as the urge to be creative, become associated with the feeling of pleasure. It is this that keeps us using these tendencies. Furthermore, the feeling of pleasure is so firmly associated with our creativity that we gain pleasure in creative hobbies just as we do in biologically useful creative activity.

The creative hobby, which we enjoy, expands our creativity in other fields of life. In fact we gain in all ways. If our working life is routine, as it is for so many of us, our creative hobby can provide what is otherwise missing. We gain pleasure because we are exercising our minds in a way which has been biologically advantageous in the past. More than this, our creative hobby often acts as a learning experience. In the hobby we give our mind free rein. It is no longer harnessed by rigid restraints. It learns a greater freedom of action. This, without our conscious awareness, is carried over so that we come to deal with the affairs of our day to day life more freely and in more creative fashion.

Artistic hobbies help us understand the essential harmony of nature which surrounds us and of which we ourselves are part. The individual may not see it quite like this. He may simply say, 'I like my art. I enjoy it. Somehow it is a challenge. I feel better for doing it.' Why does he like it? Why does he enjoy it? Why is it a challenge? Why does he feel better for doing it? From early times we have had glimpses of the harmony of nature. The seasons come and go; there is a time for sowing and a time for harvest; children are born; their parents die; the children have further offspring. These are the very obvious manifestations of essential harmony. We observe these things. We feel that there is more. And in our artistic hobbies, through the shape and form and colour and light of what we create, we give these feelings some kind of expression, vague and incomplete though it be.

Reading can be escapist, informative or cultural. The present tendency is towards the escapist and the informative. Our escapist literature is easily recognised, but we may in fact read informative material for purely escapist purposes. We read the evening paper just as much to escape from our problems as to be informed about the events of the day. On the other hand we are becoming very conscious of wasting our time, and our reading of the more serious novels has turned to those written on a background of historical, social, political or technical information so that the reader is left with the feeling of gaining something informative although he is only reading fiction.

Cultural reading brings our mind to a higher level of functioning. By cultural reading I do not refer to reading about cultural topics which I would classify as informative. In cultural reading our mind is led into new patterns of thought and feeling which are beyond those of our ordinary life. The author's clear expression of ideas brings our own mind to a similar clarity of thought. By identification with the characters we ourselves come to experience deeper and more human emotions. Through the interaction of the characters we gain understanding of problems which otherwise eludes us. We gain from such reading; but the thought content of what we read need not exclusively concern good acts or emotions. In fact the theme of cultural literature may concern great evil as is the case in many of the tragic dramas. We gain through the psychological reactions which such reading induces.

We can gain through cultural reading, likewise we can be debased through certain types of reading. Let us look at it this way. In the early days of our race we could only use our minds in vague and simple fashion. We have gradually developed the ability to think more clearly and more logically. We have developed shades of feeling which were previously unknown to us. In the past we were concerned with our own personal survival, now we have come to think more of others. We experienced crude emotions, such as hostility, fear and lust, which helped us in our immediate struggle. Now we are gradually learning to feel more of love and compassion. On this background let us examine our reading habits. We gain from cultural reading which brings us, either directly or indirectly, something of these newer and more truly human aspects of life. On the other hand, we are debased if our reading brings us back to experience those more primitive thoughts and feelings, which we should have outgrown by the process of evolution.

Why do we have such a liking for that type of reading which debases us? I think the answer lies in the matters which we have just discussed. All our reactions which have been of biological value to us become tinged with the feeling of pleasure. We like the experience of these reactions. It is this that brings us to use them. In the past those of us who did not like these reactions did not use them and so failed to survive. Those who liked the feeling of aggression could fight better. Those who liked lust had more children. Now we have developed similar feelings towards love and compassion; but the old liking for the primitive emotions still lingers on. 'I like a good fight.' So we like debasing literature on account of the primitive pleasure it can still give us in this way. To enhance our quality of life we need to choose our reading so that our pleasure comes from the experience of the good feeling associated with our newer and more humanistic emotions. Many read debasing literature for escapist purposes. It takes the mind off the real problem. We must understand, of course, all escapist reading is not debasing.

There is another point. I think I can explain it best by an example. Yesterday morning I saw a young doctor as a patient. He is very sensitive, very idealistic, in fact a very good doctor. With great shame he said, 'I have a craving for pornography'. He had upset his young wife by trying to explain the problem to her. After talking with him for a little while it became clear that the urge for pornography only came upon him when he was tense. The tension might come from any cause, problems in his medical practice, difficulties with the children or sexual conflicts with his wife. I have seen other patients like this. When they learned how to reduce their tension, the urge for pornography ceased. I think it will be the same with this young doctor.

In the portrayal of violence the theatre and the film may add to the quality of our life or detract from it. A tendency to violence is a part of our biological heritage and it is always near at hand in our great cities. Sex is an integral part of our life. The more we understand of these matters the better it is for us. So we want to be informed about the realities of life. But we identify with the actors and so become emotionally involved ourselves. In our evolutionary past in order to survive we needed an ability to act violently. To act violently we needed a capacity to be cruel. Without this our capacity for violence would have been so much the less. From our stone age existence, through primitive hunting life and simple agrarian communities, we have evolved to a better stage of life in which we no longer have a need for violence to survive. If the play directly or indirectly evokes in us a disgust for violence and a compensating feeling of compassion, the experience is helping us towards a more fully human way of life. However, if the violence is depicted in such a way that our latent violent reactions are alerted and our primitive tendency to cruelty becomes mobilised, the experience of seeing the play has an adverse effect upon us through re-activating primitive reactions in place of the more humanistic and compassionate ones which we are gradually learning.

Sex on the screen or stage may lead us to a better life or it may debase us. It is not the nakedness, nor the display of the sexual organs, nor actual intercourse which determines whether we are uplifted or debased. It is the attitude of the lovers.

In our very primitive, stone age days, sex was basically a physiological function. If the film presents sexual intercourse as a purely physiological act, we are debased because our identification with the participants reactivates our more primitive sexual feelings. On the other hand this effect may be negated by showing that one or both partners are debased by such an experience. But if the sexual act on the stage is used to express love and tenderness in a more complete way than is our own ordinary experience, then witnessing it is something uplifting as it helps us on the way to a fuller experience of these emotions in our own life.

As we have seen, leisure plays an important part in our lives adding to the quality of life and our physical well-being. Our leisure can lead us to repose, but we must remember that repose in itself is more than mere inactivity. People who are constantly tense with a high level of anxiety find it difficult to attain even moments of repose. In fact, I see many people professionally whom I am sure have never had the experience of real repose. To them it is as distant as walking on the moon, and as in-comprehensible as higher mathematics are to most of us. I believe that our modern way of life contributes to this with its restless need to be constantly doing things.

However, we can ameliorate the situation by reducing our level of nervous tension by Mental Ataraxis. Many people who have practised this have told me how they have gained through the moments of repose which now come spontaneously.

13

STRESS IN OUR LIFE

Stress is the disparity between the demands made upon us and our ability to cope with them. Stress is not the problems with which we are faced. It is always the relationship between our problems and our ability to cope with them. If the demands made upon us are great, we are more likely to be under stress. When we reduce the practical demands made upon us by a holiday, or an easier job, our stress is so much the less. If we cope well, stress is minimal; if we cope badly, stress is at a maximum. Stress is the result of the balance between these two factors.

In our ordinary life we tend to emphasise the importance of the problem and to neglect the importance of our ability to cope. Let us take extreme examples. The commander of an army in battle need not be under great stress if his training and personality integration is such that he can cope. Similarly the pilot of an aeroplane with engine trouble, provided he knows what to do and is unafraid of death. So also the girl who has been jilted if she has sufficient philosophy about her to understand; or even a woman who has just lost her family in an accident may have such religious faith that she is still able to cope. On the other hand, the day to day problems of the office may produce significant stress in someone who is less well integrated. Similarly the daily problems of getting the children to school may produce stress in the suburban housewife who does not cope well with these matters.

The danger from stress is that it produces anxiety. We have discussed the way in which anxiety arises when our brain is unable to integrate all the nervous impulses arriving at any one time. As with stress, this is a relationship phenomenon. The relationship between the number and intensity of the impulses, and our brain's capacity for integrating them. When we think of stress, we are really viewing the same situation from a humanistic point of view rather than that of neurophysiology.

We can reduce stress by increasing our capacity to cope through the practice of Mental Ataraxis. I see examples of this every day. A businessman deals with the same problems without stress. A woman with an alcoholic husband now copes with the situation.

A student copes with his studies which were previously producing stress. A girl copes with the uncertainties of an unfaithful lover. And so on. When we practise Mental Ataraxis we increase our capacity to cope with our problems. The disparity between the demands made upon us and our ability to cope with them is reduced and we live our life with less stress.

We cope with the demands made upon us by both practical doing and inner psychological adjustment. If the boss is difficult we have to cope by doing things his way; but if we are to avoid stress we must also make inner psychological adjustments so that our doing things his way does not arouse our aggression. If we do things his way but at the same time bottle up our own hostile feelings, we are not coping effectively and in consequence we are under stress. On the other hand, if we do things his way, and at the same time retain an ease of mind about us without getting fussed, we are coping in mature fashion and the demand upon us has not produced stress.

The demands made upon us, with which we must cope and which contribute to our stress, often arise in areas that we do not suspect. We are likely to think in terms of increased work load or the consequences of some sudden accident or emotional deprivation. The businessman thinks of the decisions he must make. The housewife is aware of the demands the children make upon her in terms of her need for patience. Young people are constantly confronted with the demands of study. We can see how these realistic matters contribute to our stress. But there are other more intangible factors the significance of which often eludes us.

Whatever our lifestyle there are emotional demands made upon us with which we must cope. We have to cope with the mood of those around us. The mood of the boss at work makes demands upon us. So does the mood of our wife or husband at home. This may be sensed as irritability, depression, or simply as remoteness. Whatever the mood of the other, it makes demands upon us and so contributes to our stress.

We have to cope with the demands of our love life and our other basic appetites. This goes for all of us. Do we cope well with our basic sexual urge which can become so easily aroused in inappropriate circumstances as well as those that are appropriate? Do we cope well with our inner need to integrate our basic sexual urge with love and tender feelings? What of our other simple appetites? Do we cope well with our body's demand for food and drink, or do we find it difficult to moderate our eating and drinking, and so come under stress?

Our body itself makes demands upon us. When we are tired can we cope, and still work at ease in spite of our tiredness, or in these circumstances do we have to drive ourselves to continue to work and so come under stress? If our work should involve discomfort or even pain, can we continue in a relaxed state of mind to do what has to be done, or do we come under stress by continually fighting in our mind against the situation?

Our own inner psychic life makes very real demands upon us with which we must cope. We have within us a sense of duty making demands upon us which are just as real and just as compelling as the demands of our boss at work or the children at home. Our conscience makes demands upon us, and when these are not met we feel the goading prods of guilt about us.

However beyond duty and conscience we have a sense of idealism which also makes demands upon us. Different people experience it in different ways. To some sport-loving Australians it may be no more than a sense of fair play. To others it is a feeling of compassion for fellow man, and for others it extends into a sense of the mystical, but it is there in one form or another in most of us; and it makes demands upon us in the sense of need to fulfil this feeling within us.

The demands of our inner life take many forms. For instance there is the demand for completion, to finish the job, to tidy it up. If in fact we can bring the task to completion our mind has a better chance of resting at ease. I am more than usually aware of this reaction at the moment, as I am just finishing this manuscript. However, in the reality of life it often happens that we are in fact unable to complete the matter. In these circumstances our psychological adjustment must be such that we can accept the fact of the uncompleted task without resultant nervous tension. We are then coping well and stress is minimal.

Some of the demands with which we must cope are associated with our modern way of life. These are important because they are new to us and in the biological sense we have not had much experience in dealing with them.

The very fact of living in a city makes certain demands upon us. For instance we must learn to conform, as a high degree of conformity helps us to live closely together in harmony with each other. Permissiveness and understanding also help, and are, in fact, a superior way of adjusting to city life. However, as yet most of us have not acquired these attributes to any great extent, so for the present, city life demands that we conform. In general, the young people among us do not cope well with this demand which society makes of them, and as a result they are under stress.

City life also demands of us a kind of impersonality. In essence it is a demand that we go about our own business without too much notice of what others are doing. This is necessary. If we were to become too concerned about the problems of so many other people we would be unable to get on with our own affairs. Of course this also means that the stranger to the city finds it hard to make the friends which he needs to satisfy his gregarious needs. So city life often demands that the individual live in comparative isolation, and as a result he has to cope with the problem of loneliness.

City life demands that we learn to live without any intimate contact with nature. We are thus deprived of something which has been an intimate part of our life for hundreds of generations. The modern city dweller must cope with this demand both in the way of substitute satisfactions and psychological adjustment to the situation.

In modern life, through the consensus of those about us, we are subject to the demand to drive ourselves on to materialistic achievement. There are very few of us indeed who are free from this demand. Many feel that they are free, and they rationalise, saying that they pursue their occupation with single-minded purpose just because they like it that way. 'Materialism', as I see it, is the process by which we do things for material reward rather than for motives of idealism or inner satisfaction. Of course there is nothing new in materialism; but our present society puts pressures on us to conduct our lives in accordance with this principle. Whether or not this demand produces stress depends on our ability to cope with it without inner tension in ourselves. If we go along with the materialistic demands without inner conflict we are not under stress. However, if we break away into a more humanistic and idealistic pattern of living we must be able to do so without tension if we are to avoid stress.

The disruption of family life makes demands upon us with which we must cope. When they marry, most young people now have the vague feeling that it may not be for life. This imposes some degree of uncertainty and insecurity, particularly on the girl. The alternative, cohabitation, imposes similar uncertainties. Then with the break-up of the marriage the girl is faced with the demand that she cope with the children. Her difficulties are increased by the fact that her parents may not have a stable home where they can take her in and help her.

Of course the disruption of family life demands of young people that they become self-sufficient at an early age. This may occur at a time when they find it hard to cope psychologically. But it is the older people who are perhaps faced with the greatest demands through disrupted family life. Their adult children are no longer prepared to care for them in the family home, and they are largely left to fend for themselves and cope as best they can.

The changing status of woman makes new demands upon her
She is set to be mistress of her own destiny rather than have the pattern of her life determined by her husband. The situation makes demands on her in the way of decision making. There is also the demand that she reconcile the aggression mobilised in her competitive work life with the passivity which she needs in coping at home with the children. There is the demand that her increasing use of logic should not destroy that native empathy by which women understand the needs of their children before they can express themselves logically.

Perhaps even more important is the demand inherent in doing new things. The modern woman is actively changing her status. She is doing new things. Things which her older sister would not have dared to do. But when we are doing new things we are not as secure as when we are doing the old accustomed routines. Insecurity begets anxiety. So the modern woman, or the woman who espouses the lifestyle of the modern woman, of necessity lives with a higher level of anxiety than her sister who follows the more traditional role of woman.

As a result the modern woman with her higher level of anxiety experiences greater nervous tension, greater irritability and a greater tendency to psychosomatic disorders. However un-palatable it may be, this is a fact of life. It means that there is a demand upon the modern woman to cope with a higher level of anxiety than that of her more traditionally orientated elder sister. A solution which can resolve this apparent impasse lies in the practice of Mental Ataraxis, so that the modern woman can do new things which involve insecurity and still retain her ease of mind.

Our loss of religious faith makes demands on us, and if we do not cope adequately with the demand we are under stress. The demand is for something with which to replace our religious faith. Different people meet the demand in different ways. Some turn to rationalism and become atheist. Some feel that they can fill in the gap with their own inner philosophy without turning to some new belief. There is a turn to mysticism by an increasing number of people, while others are finding new faith in awareness of the essential rhythm of nature. If we cope with the demand for some new inner belief or personal philosophy we avoid stress, but if our coping is inadequate to the extent that we remain beset by doubts on these matters, then we know that our loss of religious faith does in fact produce stress.

We must remember that our coping with the demands made upon us always involves our psychological adjustment to the situation if we are to avoid stress. Doing the right thing in itself is not sufficient. We can do the right thing in response to the demands of the boss, the restlessness of the children or the need to study, but we avoid stress only if we do so with ease in our own mind. It is the same with the inner demands of our sense of duty and conscience. We do the right thing, we visit the sick relative, we have resisted the temptation of slightly understating our income to the tax authorities. We have done the right thing, but if in doing it we become tense in ourselves, we have not coped well with the demands made upon us and we are still under stress.

The disparity between the demands made upon us and our ability to cope is reduced, and stress is consequently less as we move towards the integration of maturity. In other words, a mature person is one who copes well. So even when considerable demands are made upon him he is still not under stress.

Whatever the origin of the demands made upon us, whether they are from the practical problems of our working life or from the inner recesses of our mind we cope with them better if we reduce our anxiety through Mental Ataraxis. This is the practical reward of what I have been writing about. In itself it is a very great reward. To cope better with the demands of life. But let us not forget those other things which go with it. The intangibles. The distant lights of which we have seen only glimpses. And the stillness, and the depth. And the move toward fulfilment of our inner being. For this is truly the Discipline of Ease.

PART THREE

The More Distant Horizon

Understanding comes to us

We use Mental Ataraxis to bring natural order to our inner life which, in turn, helps us achieve a naturally ordered material life. We have tapped the *Wealth Within.*

14

THE THEORETICAL BASIS OF MENTAL ATARAXIS

This book is intended as a practical guide, but our self-help is more complete if we understand something of the theoretical considerations upon which it is based.

Anxiety more than anything else reduces the quality of our life. I cannot emphasise this too strongly. Anxiety spoils our experience of life through nervous tension and apprehension. It makes us insecure in our work and in our interpersonal relations. It causes all our psychosomatic disorders and discomforts. It forces us into defensive distortions of our personality so that we are a lesser person than we might be.

Anxiety results when our brain is unable to integrate all the nervous impulses coming into it. Some of these impulses come through sight and sound from the environment around us. Some arise in all the various organs of our body. Some arise in our brain itself, both from the conscious thoughts in our mind about the problems which we face, and from the activity of repressed ideas in our unconscious mind of which we have no awareness of all. If our brain cannot fully integrate all these impulses, we experience anxiety.

Anxiety alerts our physiological defence mechanisms in a way that is inappropriate to our present state of evolution. Our body reacts to anxiety with increased heart rate, increased blood pressure, increased flow of blood to the muscles and many other reactions which would prepare us for physical activity.

This was an appropriate reaction at an earlier stage of evolution when the cause of anxiety was most often associated with an increase of nervous impulses due to the threat of external danger. But now, most of the threats which produce the increase in nervous impulses, are very much more subtle. The threats, in the form of worry and uncertainty, arise within the mind itself, and the preparation for physical activity is a quite inappropriate response to this new type of threatening situation.

Anxiety also acts as a warning that all is not well with us, but in fact the warning has the effect of increasing our anxiety. The feeling of apprehension is an integral part of the anxiety reaction. It clearly has its biological purpose as a warning to us that something is wrong. But with anxiety we are usually unable to see what is wrong, and if we cannot see what is wrong we are unable to do anything about it. So the warning signal, which in the past fulfilled a useful purpose by alerting us to external danger, has now come to do more harm than good.

The common belief that we need some anxiety to make us do things reflects a low level concept of life. The idea is that the uncomfortable feeling of anxiety motivates us to get going and do things. Fear also makes us do what we should do, but it is a second class motivation for behaviour. So also, guilt makes us do what we should do, but it is a second class way of living when we do things out of guilt. I believe that the same applies to anxiety.

Our mind has the capacity to reduce anxiety provided the right circumstances are provided. This is something of great significance, and I have abundant evidence in my clinical records to show beyond all doubt that it is in fact true. It means that the endless pursuit of childhood conflicts in orthodox psychotherapy is quite unnecessary. Some years ago, when I used to put forward this idea, the orthodox psychiatrists would always reply by saying that my cures would only be temporary and the patients would soon relapse. However, I have now lived long enough to know that this does not happen, and those who learn to reduce their anxiety by act of their own mind can look forward to lasting relief.

The stillness of the mind in Mental Ataraxis provides the right circumstances for our mind to reduce anxiety. Other reparative functions of the body cannot operate unless the right circumstances are provided. Our body cannot repair a broken bone unless we immobilise the pieces in the right position. We need physical rest to allow our body to repair the damage of a coronary heart attack. So it is with anxiety. Our mind needs that type of stillness which is readily attained in Mental Ataraxis.

The effects of the stillness of our mind persist after our meditation ceases. People are aware of this in varying degree. After their first experience of Mental Ataraxis it is common for patients to say that they had an unusual ease and effortlessness about them for the rest of the day. With greater experience of Mental Ataraxis the post-meditative ease of mind becomes more and more pronounced and of longer and longer duration. It is this persistence of the effect of our meditation which brings it to reduce our anxiety and to influence our life as a whole.

The stillness of Mental Ataraxis is brought about by psychological regression. This is quite a normal reaction, and most of us experience it from time to time in our moments of reverie when our mind just wanders pleasantly and aimlessly while we ourselves cease to be aware of our immediate surroundings.

Regression is a going back of the mind to an earlier mode of functioning. As a result of evolution, we are constantly developing a more and more complex brain and more and more subtle ways of using our mind. We can think in more sophisticated fashion than could Neanderthal Man. Regression is a going back to earlier and simpler ways of using our mind. There is also another type of regression in which we go back to the simpler mental processes of childhood. We see this in some people when they get frustrated and cannot cope with a situation in adult fashion. They go back to a childhood way of obtaining what they want by reacting with a tantrum or a display of emotion.

The regression of Mental Ataraxis is towards the mode of functioning of the primitive rather than that of the child. My evidence for this lies not only in my experience with hundreds of meditating patients, but also with patients in hypnosis. There is a similarity in the regression of meditation to that seen in hypnosis. The essence of hypnosis, as I have pointed out in detail in my text book *A System Of Medical Hypnosis*, is atavistic regression or regression towards primitive functioning.

The meditator experiences regression as the loss of logical thinking, dulling of perception and the loss of awareness of his immediate surroundings. But the knowledge that he has had this experience only comes after he has made the counter-regression back to normal thinking.

This is obvious, as we cannot examine our state of mind logically at a time when our logical thinking is in abeyance. It is in retrospect that we realise our mind had not been thinking about anything very much. We heard some noises, but they did not seem to have any particular significance, and for the time being we had really forgotten where we were. When ideas such as these come to us, we know that we have emerged from a state of regression.

Regression is creative in that it allows us to see things in their innate simplicity. Ideas come to us without the trappings with which we habitually cover them. There is naked truth in the ideas that come to our mind. We can think in simple terms, and we feel in untarnished fashion so that it has a simplicity and purity about it. As our mind comes to work in simple fashion, we have better understanding of the essential core of our being and our place in nature, so that life and death, the seasons and the essential rhythm of things about us all come to have a meaning which previously eluded us. A thirty-three-year-old artist explained that Mental Ataraxis had provided 'a way of life which I did not think possible'.

Regression is creative in that it puts a stop to inferior and inappropriate patterns of thought and feeling, and by bringing us back to solid foundations allows better patterns to emerge. We cannot use our faulty patterns of reaction as a foundation on which to build. We cannot develop a better way of life until we first go back to something simple, and then move forward again. Regression allows us to wipe out faulty and inappropriate patterns of response and to build again on something solid.

Regression is creative in the way that it allows us true insights into ourself by dulling our normal psychological defences which ordinarily prevent us seeing ourselves as we really are. Our mind does not let us see ourselves as we really are because it would hurt us too much. It would humiliate us. So we deny, rationalise and make excuses for what we do and things about ourselves. Because of these unconscious defences we cannot see ourselves as perceptive people about us can see us. But as we regress these psychological defences become dulled and cease to operate effectively. We come to see ourselves more as we really are. And most important, the calm and ease that accompanies our regression allows this insight to come to us without causing the hurt and mental turmoil which would otherwise be the case.

Regression is creative in that we are no longer afraid to let our thoughts and feelings venture into the unknown. This comes about through the reduction of anxiety. We are secure in our inner self. When we are secure we can let our mind venture into new experiences of thought and feeling. This comes to different people in different degree, but we can all move in this direction. People who have experienced this have often spoken of the way in which they had previously been frightened to give their mind a free rein as it were.

Regression is creative in that it frees our mind from the constriction of logic. Sometimes it is hard for us to realise the extent to which logical thinking dominates our mental processes and so inhibits the creative breakthrough. Of course we need logic. An abundance of logic. But we also need moments of freedom from its constraints. As long as we allow ourselves to be held to the pedestrian steps of logic, we cannot make the creative jump forwards on to new ground.

Regression is creative to the human personality, as the reduction of anxiety which it induces frees us from the need of defensive distortions of our personality. Perhaps this is the greatest creativity that can come to us. It does not happen all at once. But I have seen many people whose personality has changed in significant fashion following the practice of Mental Ataraxis. Without exception the change has always been towards greater freedom, and openness with a lessening of those personality traits which motivate the individual towards protective, egocentric and selfish patterns of behaviour.

Regression is creative in that it accelerates the evolutionary process by dulling established patterns of reaction, and so allowing newer patterns to emerge. In this way regression allows the development of new capacities of the mind. A firmly-established aggressive reaction inhibits the development of compassion which is a more recently evolved mode of response.

In a similar way our established pattern of using our mind logically, inhibits the emergence of intuitive thought and empathic feeling which we are only just developing. Regression disrupts our established patterns of functioning and so permits us new experiences by allowing these emergent abilities to function freely. I have emphasised the importance of regression because so many people experienced in meditation, Yoga and Zen have reacted in hostile fashion when I have spoken of these practices as involving regression. They have immediately assumed that any going back is retrograde in the sense of being bad. This of course is not so.

In the march of our evolutionary progress to things better, we move forward, then back a little to consolidate and then forward again. Without these backward steps real progress is impossible. The regression of Mental Ataraxis allows us these momentary respites and so hastens our progress to a more fully human experience of life.

Mental Ataraxis allows the spontaneous development of more idealistic value systems. This is often shown by the meditator seeking some more humanitarian or socially useful form of occupation or engaging in part time activity of a charitable nature. It may show in his expressed attitudes to members of his family or people at work. More often this change in value systems has come to my notice through comments by members of the patient's family or workmates. The change is always from more material values to more idealistic values. I believe that this comes about as a result of the general reduction of anxiety.

This is a strange reaction. In times past, when man has become threatened and anxious he has traditionally turned to his God and more idealistic value systems. This was where he put his faith, and by this means he was reassured; but things have changed. Now, when we are threatened, we put our faith in the security of material things. When we become less anxious, we are not so closely bound to material things, and we allow the development of more idealistic values.

Another interesting aspect of this reaction is that the turn to more idealistic values is quite spontaneous and does not follow from any direct or indirect suggestions from me. It just comes of itself, as part of the more fully human experience of life which follows Mental Ataraxis.

15

BEYOND RELAXATION

*The full meditative experience is beyond the relaxation of the body
and mind, beyond the transcendence of discomfort.* What is it then?
Is it something strange and unnatural? No. There is nothing
strange or bizarre about it at all. Nor is there anything dramatic
or exciting. Do not expect ecstasy or any outlandish distortions
of the mind. Expect rather the experience of deep naturalness.
Utter naturalness. It is only when this comes to us that we realise
that true naturalness is something quite foreign to us in our
ordinary lives. Simplicity. Such profound simplicity that we are
almost overwhelmed by it, immersed in it.

> I wrote this a few days ago and I am just reading it over
> again. This morning I saw as a patient, a twenty-three-year-
> old married speech therapist. It was her third session and
> she is already much less tense. As she left, she looked at me
> and said, 'It is the utter simplicity of it.'

*Words fail. We can only fully understand meditation by experiencing
it.* This is true. But it should not deter us in our quest as we
can understand many other human experiences only when we
have experienced them. Many years ago I had been discussing
meditation with a very old and saintly yogi in the Himalayas.
One morning he said to me, 'You can show a child a banana,
but you cannot tell him how it tastes.' This is a profound truth.
And of course this is so with meditation.
It is easy to become confused by the simplicity of the procedure
and what seems to be an absence of a logical basis. A fifty-year-
old consulting engineer had complained of nervous tension and
poor sleep. After two sessions he stated that he had had an
extraordinary weekend skiing in which he felt completely relaxed
in a way that he had never before experienced. Then he said
that he could not accept this form of treatment as it was irrational
and he had decided to discontinue. However he later resumed
treatment and has remained off sleeping pills for two years after
taking them for twenty-five years. He has also achieved inter-
national professional success which he attributes to his greater
ease of mind and clarity of thought.

Then there was the manageress of a frock shop who said, 'I've been a lot different since coming here. Can't understand the change when you don't tell us anything. You haven't told me how to think differently, but I am thinking differently.'

Although it is often hard to explain what has happened to us, we can, nevertheless, discuss some general principles which can be expressed and which are helpful in the understanding of the experience.

In meditation we can let our mind experience ideas. This may seem rather strange. In our ordinary waking life we think ideas, we do not experience them. I am attempting to describe to you a process of very great simplicity, but at the same time of very great importance. It is rather a matter of an awareness of the ideas. A very simple awareness. It is in much the same way as we are often aware of another person in the room without actually thinking that he is there with us. We just seem to experience an awareness of the other person. In a similar kind of way we can experience ideas in our meditation.

It helps us to experience ideas in meditation if we first think about the ideas before we meditate. This thinking about the ideas prior to meditation is an ordinary process of logical thought. We just think about them quietly and quite naturally. Then when we come to meditate, we cease to think in the ordinary way, and by a very simple process of our mind we can bring ourselves simply to experience awareness of the ideas. Then, as our meditation proceeds, other ideas come to our awareness. These other ideas are related to those which we were originally thinking about. But the relationship is not a logical one. It is paralogical. In this way the new ideas may bring us flashes of insight which are beyond us in our ordinary waking state.

It helps if we start by experiencing fairly tangible ideas such as our own inner ease. Of course, our inner ease is really an abstraction and is not tangible at all; but it is not too difficult to let our mind endow our inner ease with tangible qualities. We can feel our body at ease, this is tangible enough. The next step is to experience the ease of our body as part of ourself. Then we have the experience of our own inner ease. And of course it is not a matter of repeating the idea of it to ourselves, or thinking about it, or examining it, or contemplating it. It is just simply experiencing it. As it comes to us, we can let our mind go further so that the experiencing of it becomes something quite wonderful.

We experience the letting go of ourself. This involves a sense of freedom, of very great freedom, defencelessness, of completely letting go, of utter abandonment. There is a sense of real abandonment. But the abandonment is not disordered. It is as if we give direction to our sense of abandonment. Without this we would experience chaos and the disintegration of our mind. But the complete abandonment together with a sense of direction allows us to experience ideas in simplicity and purity without distortion from our usual protective psychological reactions.

Besides the letting go of ourself, there is also a deeper process of simply 'letting ourself'. In this state of 'letting ourself' we come to experience aspects of our being which we do not ordinarily experience. This idea is probably quite foreign to you and may be a little difficult to grasp. But it is both very simple and very important. Normally our psychological protective mechanisms prevent us from experiencing 'letting ourself.' But in the meditative state, and the reduction of anxiety which goes with it, the 'letting ourself' is quite safe. Through it we come to experience aspects of our being which are otherwise inaccessible to us, and our mind learns in the process.

We come to the experience of letting our mind learn. Our daily life is a sequence of experiences. One after the other. If we think about this, we soon see that we really learn very little from these experiences of daily life. Yes, occasionally we do learn something. When we make some glaring mistake and we learn not to do the same thing again. But in general we learn very little from our daily experiences. There are many reasons for this. We have a certain defensive rigidity about us, a basic conservatism, which works to keep us doing things the same old way and makes us cling to the same old patterns of reaction. We don't learn from our daily experiences in the way that we should. But in our meditative relaxation there is this deep 'letting of ourself'. A kind of freedom of our being. In this state we are not held back in the way that we usually are, and our mind learns from experience in a way that is normally impossible. This not only applies to our mind learning both from the meditative experience itself and the various facets of experience which go with it, but it also applies by way of increasing our ability to let our mind learn from our experiences of everyday life.

In the letting go of Mental Ataraxis we experience the inner freedom that is part of our being. Many stories of martyrdom tell us how inner freedom has come while the limbs have been shackled. We can achieve this effect in simple form in our meditation. There is an experience of freedom. We are free inwardly. Our mind learns in the experience. We are able to cast off the ties which constrict our thought and feeling in ordinary life.

A sensitive forty-five year old woman patient of mine had complained of nervous tension of more than twenty years duration. She had spent many years trying to gain ease of mind in Yoga and Zen practice. Later she wrote a letter of thanks, 'Thank you for capturing for me that elusive, gossamer wing of serenity that defies description: something for which I have searched for so long but apparently in the wrong way, it has always been just out of reach.'

The inner freedom of meditative experience allows expression of our creativity. In our waking life we have been pondering the problem, thinking about it, and feeding into our mind all the relevant facts. But no solution comes. In these circumstances it is not uncommon for the answer to come to us in meditation. Our mind is free from its usual constraints. We are no longer thinking of the problem. Our mind is still and free. In the tranquillity of this state relevant ideas become associated, and with no thought or effort or striving on our part the answer just comes to us. As a woman muscian said, 'I now have a completely different slant on musical perception.'

When we are really relaxed our interpersonal relationships become easy in a way which was not otherwise possible. Such has been the discovery of so many different people from various walks of life – people like a public servant who came for help with sweating and blushing. Later he said, 'Feel fine...a few beaut days... kind of naturalness about it...Because you are more relaxed you get along with other people', or the tense married woman of forty-two who had come to me on account of sex difficulty, 'Can meet people more easily and look at them when I talk to them', she explained.

A forty-five-year-old single woman librarian once said, 'Easier inside...a whole heap better...feel as I did twelve years ago.' A month later she added, 'Better and better...less worry guarding myself...less self-conscious...feel attitude to men changing...more responsive in general.'

Lastly, let me tell you about an attractive young married woman who complained of severe chronic nervous tension. She subsequently said, 'It has spread into my life without my doing

anything about it...feel a different person...new life for me...
can cope with things now.' She later wrote a letter of thanks in
which she said that she likes people better now, and has re-
captured her love of music. 'It seems that some blockage that I
had always had has been cleared away.'

We are relaxed, but we experience something far beyond relaxation.
It is our inner ease. The calm that is natural to us. It is there.
Natural to us. But at the same time it is ordinarily beyond us.
Our mind learns from the experience, and we learn. A fifty-year-
old married woman had complained that she had been very
agitated ever since she could remember. Later when speaking
of Mental Ataraxis she said, 'Getting stillness with it. A freedom.
So still, so free. Nothing holding me back like there used to be.'

Our mind learns and we learn. It is all one. We experience our
body, our mind, our inner self, our own self. But it is all one.
A complete integration. And in our meditation we experience
this integration. It is more than an integration of discrete parts.
It is wholeness. This is our being.

We started with the relaxation of individual muscles. In the
greater experience there are no individual muscles only our body
itself, and in the still greater experience there is no body and
mind, or inner self and our own self, it is just the experience of
our being.

*In our meditation we experience naturalness. It is more than the
naturalness of the meditative experience, it is the naturalness of it
all, of our own self.* A deepening and expanding sense of naturalness. There is nothing odd or strange or peculiar about it. We
experience the naturalness of what we are doing. As we become
immersed in it, the sense of naturalness spreads out, so that it is
not only what we are doing that is natural, but we are natural
in ourself. We experience our own naturalness and this enhances
our naturalness in the ordinary affairs of our everyday living.

In our meditation we experience simplicity. I must remind you
again this is not a matter of thinking about the desirability of
the quality of simplicity and how we might attain it. Nor is it
a matter of contemplating the idea of simplicity and holding the
idea of it in our mind as it were. No. I am asking you to experience simplicity. Not think about it, not contemplate it, but
to let it become a part of our being so that we experience it.
This is not too difficult. Mental Ataraxis is in fact something

very simple. We experience the simplicity of our meditation, and soon find that we are experiencing a sense of our own simplicity. The process deepens. It soon becomes more than a sense of simplicity. It is simplicity itself. We are it. It is us. Not the sensation, not a quality that we take on, but the thing itself. The effect of the experience lingers on. We come to grasp things in their basic simplicity, so that the fundamentals are no longer obscured by the paraphernalia with which we dress them.

In our meditation we experience something of the natural harmony of things. In ordinary life, when we care to, we can think about the natural harmony of the universe, and closer at hand, the natural harmony of nature as we see it in our daily life. But we rarely experience this harmony as part of ourself. This, of course, is a gross failure on our part, as we are ourselves obviously a part, however small, of the great picture. I think the reason for our failure to participate in the essential harmony around us is that our inherent anxiety prevents us. When we are tense our sense of the harmony of things is disrupted. I believe that this applies to all of us, as I have learned that those who claim an absence of nervous tension, do in fact have a level of anxiety which is quite easily demonstrable clinically. Now, when we come to meditate it is quite different. In the stillness of mind that is part of it all anxiety has gone. It is in this profound calm that the sense of harmony comes to us. Then as we go further, it is no longer just a sense of harmony. It becomes the experience of harmony so that we, body and mind and our whole being, are participating in it.

The experience beyond relaxation comes to us as an awareness that our life process has taken on a new dimension. We experience life in a different way. There is simplicity of such depth that it brings a new experience of life. It is a sense of being. Just being in its purest form. It is only after Mental Ataraxis that some people come to realise how tense they were previously. They had become so accustomed to a second class experience of life that they accepted it as normal.

The experience that our life process has taken on a new dimension comes to different people in different ways. To some it is a quasi-religious experience. Only yesterday I saw a young man of twenty-nine who first came to me on account of migraine headaches which he said he had had since the age of four. The headaches were often triggered off by stress and were frequently so severe that he would have to call the doctor who would give him an injection to help relieve the pain. Yesterday when he came in I wrote down his exact words, 'I believe I am cured. Have been getting closer to God. Almost free of headaches.' He went on to explain that he felt that the meditative experience which I had shown him had helped him to get closer to God. This was how he felt although there was nothing religious about the way I had shown him how to experience the relaxing meditation.

A Christian woman consulted me because she had been tense as long as she could remember. After two sessions she said, 'I have been feeling marvellous, much more at ease.' Two months later she looked me squarely in the face and said, 'It's really a spiritual experience, isn't it.'

A Jewish woman said after Mental Ataraxis, 'It was like a little miracle. No medication at all.'

In the experience beyond relaxation there is complete freedom from anxiety. This in itself is a new experience of life for almost all of us. We all live our daily lives on the background of anxiety. The curse of civilised man. We do not know where we are going. Some have faith. But it is never complete, never utterly complete. So anxiety lingers with us. With some it is at a high level, with others fluctuating, and with a few it is just there and that is all. Just the background noise of anxiety that restlessly churns the mind and keeps the soul from complete ease. But, in the experience of meditation, this background of anxiety fades. There is a calm which we do not experience in ordinary life situations, and our life takes on a new dimension of living.

In the state beyond relaxation we experience complete defenceless-ness. This again is a new dimension in living. In ordinary life it is only in sleep and in unconsciousness that we are defenceless. And even in sleep the defencelessness of our mind is not complete. We dream. But the defences of our mind are still sufficiently active to distort the meaning of our dreams so that it will not be too hurtful to us. But in meditation we are neither asleep nor unconscious. We are awake, but calm, and defenceless.

The defencelessness of our mind in the experience beyond relaxation has a profound effect on us. It is a new experience. It is only then that we can know ourselves. We don't know ourselves in the sense of logical knowing because in deep meditation our logical faculties have ceased to function. Rather it is that we come to know ourselves through experiencing ourselves in our new state of defencelessness. We cannot truly know ourselves, either logically or by experience, if our psychological defences are still active because we then know ourselves only as beings distorted by these defences. We can understand this process more clearly by thinking of some of our friends and considering the way in which they know themselves. It is clear that even those of us who think about such matters have quite distorted views of what we are like both mentally and spiritually. But in meditation we experience ourselves as we are. Defenceless. Our true self.

The defencelessness of our mind brings trust. A tendency to be untrusting has been bred into us. In our tribal life those of us who were not too trusting of their fellows had a greater likelihood of survival. This inherited tendency is soon reinforced by the child's early experience of life. But to be untrusting is something less than a fully human experience of life. When we trust we are not only freer in ourselves, but our trust evokes reciprocal trust in others. In the defencelessness of deep meditation a greater capacity to trust comes to us.

The experience of psychological defencelessness is a move towards greater openness of our personality in ordinary life. In ordinary life none of us is completely open. We all suffer in greater or lesser degree from various constrictions and distortions of our personality. In the last analysis all these constrictions and distortions of our personality are unconscious psychological defensive manoeuvres to help us feel more secure. This is true, it does not matter what form the particular distortion takes. Thus, being fussy, being mean, being suspicious are clearly all attitudes of mind aimed at coping with anxiety. So are aggression and timidity. So are greed and selfishness. If we are free from anxiety we are secure, and there is no motivation to be aggressive or timid or greedy or selfish. In fact, all these unpleasant distortions of our personality are unconscious means of coping with our own inner insecurity. It is in this way that anxiety makes us less of a person than we might be. The defencelessness of meditation continues in lesser degree into our waking life, and so helps us towards a more fully human status.

In the experience beyond relaxation our physical identity merges with the world around us. In our ordinary waking life we feel that there is a very clear distinction between what is me and what is not me. Our physical being is clearly determined by the boundaries of our body. But in the experience of Mental Ataraxis the sharpness of this distinction is lost. We have our place with these other things around us. Like ourselves they are part of it all, and in this greater picture the boundaries between ourself and these other things seems less important. It comes to be a matter of no importance at all. In fact there is nothing between us and these other things, and our physical identity merges with them.

There are analogies to this phenomenon in our ordinary life. The artisan may become so adept and expert with his tool that it becomes part of his own personal identity. The bricklayer's trowel becomes part of himself, so also with the skier's skis, and of course very much more so is the violinist's bow. Even our car becomes part of ourself, and we say of the other motorist, 'He nearly hit me', when we really mean, 'He nearly hit my car.' But in meditation this extension of our physical identity becomes much wider and more diffuse.

Besides our physical identity, our personal identity also undergoes changes. We ordinarily feel our sense of identity as separate from our physical body, but somehow housed within it. Thus we speak of 'My body', and so imply that we own or possess our body. We also speak of, 'My brain, my mind, my personality, my soul', so that the seat of our identity is not confined to any physical organ, nor is it a mental abstraction of our whole body. In meditation the confines of our personal identity are expanded. There comes about a change so that we are no longer confined to our body, but are part of the world around us. It is my world just as it has been my body, and the seat of my identity is now of the world rather than my body.

We experience pure being. I have sometimes had conversations like this with people who have come to seek my help.

'You want me to try to relax.'
'No. No trying. I don't want you to do anything.'
'You want me to go to sleep.'
'No. I don't want you to go to sleep. I don't want you to do anything.'
'But you must do something.'

In the experience beyond relaxation we are not asleep, we are not unconscious, we are doing something. We are being. Just being. Not even being alive which adds another dimension to our being. We simply experience our being in pure form.

This is not too difficult. It is just that we have grown so

accustomed to the practical aspects of doing things that at first we find it hard to catch the idea of pure being. We think of ourselves as being serene, as being tranquil, as being still or as being in repose. In each case we relate our being to some other quality. In the experience of pure being this is absent. It goes beyond these concepts in its profound simplicity and utter naturalness. Just being.

In the experience beyond relaxation we come to understand our place in the natural order of things. This is not a matter of working it out in a very relaxed state of mind. We can often do this, and gain understanding of problems whose solution otherwise eludes us. But we are now considering a different process of the mind. Understanding comes to us. Then we know. We sense the meaning of things. We understand something more of the life that is going on around us. We understand our place in the great order of things in a way that we did not understand before.

You, the reader, may well ask, 'If you have had experience of this greater understanding, why don't you tell us about it?'

The answer, of course, is that this understanding does not come through reason and the logical workings of our mind, so it is not possible to describe it accurately in logical writing. Let us remember that a poet can communicate ideas by simile and metaphor that defy reasoned expression. I am trying rather to lead you into an experience, a very simple experience, and the understanding which I wish to communicate will come to you by this indirect means.

In the experience beyond relaxation the solution of specific problems often comes to us. This is different from our philosophical understanding of our place in the great scheme of things. The most common manifestation of this process comes when the individual has been wondering what he should do, which course of action he should take. It is often a matter of importance to the individual's general way of life, and it not infrequently involves some moral consideration, either directly or indirectly. It may be a decision about a change of occupation, or family life, or it may involve an affair or some other love relationship. Over the years, on very many occasions people whom I have led into the experience beyond relaxation have said to me, 'Now I know the answer to a problem which has been worrying me for a long time.' I have then asked them about the problem and the solution. A point of basic importance is that on many occasions I had not been aware of the individual's problem. This clearly shows that the solution has come about by the experience beyond relaxation and not through any indirect suggestion from myself.

As we let the experience of Mental Ataraxis come to us we feel that it is good. This comes quite naturally and spontaneously. The evidence for this is that many people make comments to this effect without my having suggested anything to them. We experience it as good. But it has become clear to me that this general feeling has a variety of different aspects.

The experience of Mental Ataraxis feels good because of our reduced level of anxiety. It feels good, we feel good. But this experience often transcends the awareness of good health and ease of mind. It is good to feel good in the sense that feeling good is our natural biological state, and when we feel good in this way, it is good because we have attained our full biological potential in this area.

In Mental Ataraxis we may experience a sense of good that lies deep within ourselves. This is something difficult to describe, but to some people it is very real. In Mental Ataraxis, with the absence of anxiety and the suspension of our psychological protective reactions, we gain a glimpse into our inner being – something which is otherwise closed to us. We experience something of ourselves which we had not previously experienced! We experience something very good – an awareness of a source of good within us.

This is exactly how some people feel it and of course this is true; true in the sense of material reality, for we all do have a capacity for good. It is just that in Mental Ataraxis we come face to face, as it were, with this natural capacity for good which is within us.

As the meditative process deepens, the repressive mechanism of the mind ceases to function effectively, and ideas which were previously repressed may flood into consciousness. In this way the meditator may gain some startling insights into his own nature. There is an important point here. A similar phenomenon occurs in hypnosis, and I found it quite a common occurrence in the days when I used to work with hypno-analysis. In hypnosis the patient may gain sudden insight into unsuspected homosexual or incestuous desires with which he cannot cope and which temporarily threaten his mental balance. Although people in

Mental Ataraxis may become aware of previously repressed ideas, the process seems to be more gradual than in hypnosis and I have never seen the disturbing reactions in Mental Ataraxis which were a common occurrence in my work with hypnosis.

As our mind relaxes we may come to experience various subjective phenomena. Other than the experience of very great calm and ease, subjective phenomena are not a part of Mental Ataraxis. However, in the very relaxed state of Mental Ataraxis it is easy enough to induce subjective phenomena. But the purpose of Mental Ataraxis is the attainment of a better life. The experience of weird subjective phenomena does not help us in this, and it has the effect of diverting our interest from our goal. Perhaps I should make one exception to this general statement. I have had a number of young people as patients who had been experimenting with hallucinogenic drugs. When I have shown them that they can induce equally vivid hallucinogenic phenomena without any drugs, a number of them have given up drug taking altogether. And as a result of this their life, both in its inner being and in practical reality, has made a great change for the better. This would seem to be a legitimate use of the hallucinogenic potentiality of deep meditation. But with this exception I always advise people to avoid these exotic subjective phenomena.

A twenty-one-year-old youth said, 'I've gained quite a lot. It's quite close to being "stoned" except better. Have gone off "pot" quite a lot. I think this way is a lot better.' A month later: 'You have shown me something I have not experienced before, like a new world. Effect it has had on my life has strengthened my character.' Two months later – 'I have been thinking about this. The main effect is that it has made me feel much more secure.'

Strange subjective phenomena cease spontaneously, unless they are purposely catalysed by act of mind. If you will ignore any strange subjective phenomena, they will soon peter out. Their demise can be accelerated by actively experiencing our own inner calm and ease.

Some people display a morbid desire to experience unusual subjective phenomena. These are usually unstable thrillseekers, and from the point of view of personality and motivation they are analogous to the takers of hallucinogenic drugs, glue sniffers, and those who experiment in antisocial acts or homosexuality just for the thrill of it. Others become lured into seeking more and more intense subjective phenomena simply through the pleasure that they derive from it, particularly in the way of changing patterns of kaleidoscopic colour. A third group of people fall into the way of inducing unusual subjective phenomena in the belief that it is a revelation of the divine. I recently had a young schizo-phrenic doctor as a patient who reported that he was experiencing extraordinary revelations from God in this way. However when I told him to concentrate on his own calm and ease of mind the revelations ceased. The important consideration is that these phenomena soon cease of their own accord unless the individual keeps activating them purposely by act of mind. I shall just briefly describe some of these phenomena so that you will not be disturbed by them should they come to you spontaneously in your early sessions of Mental Ataraxis.

The subjective phenomena of mental relaxation arise as a result of the loosening of normal control. The loosening of control is seen at three levels. First there is the matter of conscious control. In normal circumstances we control the expression of our emotions. As we relax in Mental Ataraxis we let go this conscious control. Last week a woman who had lost her son three months previously in a motor accident began to sob silently as I led her into Mental Ataraxis although she had not wept since the day of his death. She had let go the conscious effort which she had been using to control her feelings. In general this type of experi-ence is beneficial to the individual.

We are all inhibited to various degrees, introverts more so than extraverts. Our inhibitions are really a protective measure to save us from the consequences of experiencing our emotions too freely. A few days ago, after his session of Mental Ataraxis with me, a young man said he had been thinking of his boss and he had not previously realised how he really hated him. The dulling of his unconscious inhibitory processes had allowed him to experience his true feelings.

The third level of control which is loosened in Mental Ataraxis concerns repression. This is the psychological mechanism which denies us awareness of certain ideas which would disturb us too much if they were to come into our clear consciousness. A young school teacher recently told me that he had experienced homo-sexual thoughts about his brother during Mental Ataraxis. These were not new to him, but the incident gave him the opportunity to discuss the matter in objective fashion with me.

We may experience various sensations concerning our body. Of these, the most common is the feeling of floating. It is often a feeling of floating in calm. Just calmness and we are floating in it. There is great peace of mind and inner tranquillity. I believe that this phenomenon is associated with the absence of anxiety. In a way our anxiety keeps us earthbound. When free of anxiety, we lose our anchor, as it were, and we are free to float off and drift in the sea of tranquillity.

Sometimes our body may seem very big, huge, so that we tower over all that is around us. Again, I believe that this is associated with our absence of anxiety. When we are free of anxiety we are greater persons. We think big, we act big, we are big.

Occasionally people feel that their face is very big, particularly the mouth and lips. When this occurs, it is common for the hands also to be felt as very large. This strange phenomenon is due to the psychological regression which occurs in meditation. In the foetus, the face, mouth and hands are disproportionately large as compared with those of the adult, and the sensory nerve supply is proportionally much greater in these areas than the rest of the body.

It is quite common to experience various visual phenomena. Although the eyes are closed, the visual field may fill with various colours, patterns and shapes. The hue of the colours may have an unearthly quality about it. The colours change and merge from one into the other. Commonly they pulsate. There is such splendour in the colour that the individual is tempted to prolong and repeat the experience. But rather than this I would advise that you concentrate on the primary purpose of Mental Ataraxis which is the attainment of ease of mind as a step towards a better life. On rare occasions the colours take on recognisable shapes and the experience has the quality of a vivid dream or perhaps even a vision. I emphasise that these phenomena cease when we let ourselves return to the experience of our own inner ease.

Long forgotten memories of past events may flood into the mind. An unstable young doctor told me he had been using meditation for this purpose. He had been doing this partly for what he considered its therapeutic effect, and partly to satisfy his curiosity about forgotten events of his unhappy childhood. He was clearly in danger of bringing to consciousness thoughts and feelings of the past which might have been too disturbing for him to integrate in his present unstable state. When I asked him simply to let himself concentrate on his own natural ease, this flood of disturbing memories ceased.

As we commence a session of meditation we may experience dramatic changes of mood. We may find that we start in a normal state of mood, neither particularly happy nor particularly sad. Then as the meditation proceeds we may find our mind filled with sadness. This is simply due to the fact that in ordinary life we prevent ourselves thinking of our shortcomings, while in the off-guard state of early meditation these thoughts can come freely to us. More often our mood changes in the other direction. From a neutral mood we change to being extremely happy, euphoric or even ecstatic. This of course results from our experience of freedom from our habitual anxiety.

My purpose in advising against the cultivation of strange sensory phenomena is simply that an individual who is on the verge of schizophrenia could precipitate himself into the illness by this means. The experience of strange sensory phenomena in meditation is completely safe for the normal stable individual, and this warning should in no way discourage people from accepting the very great physical, mental and spiritual benefits which are so readily obtainable through meditative experience. A fundamental aspect of schizophrenia is the schizophrenic's confusion of material reality with the reality of the mind. He has difficulty in distinguishing what happens in his mind from what happens in the material world around him. The strange sensory phenomena of meditation are often very vivid and bring with them the illusion of material reality. As a result of this the young person on the verge of schizophrenia may become still further confused. The problem is accentuated by the fact that the interests of the young person who is developing schizophrenia characteristically change from the more material to the more abstract. As a result of this trend it is common for young schizophrenics to develop an interest in Yoga, Zen, and other esoteric practices involving meditation.

Although the unwise use of meditation in the way of cultivating strange phenomena can precipitate a predisposed individual into schizophrenia, the judicious use of meditation can in fact ward off schizophrenic illness. This is a matter of very considerable medical significance. I have abundant evidence to substantiate both these statements, that unwise meditation can precipitate schizophrenia, and that judicious meditation can ward off this most devastating of all illnesses. If you, the reader, have, in fact, suffered from schizophrenia or if you fear for your own inner stability, please do not embark on a course of intensive solitary meditation in an attempt to find your way back to normality. Use meditation. Use it because it can help you. But use it under the supervision of some reliable psychiatrist who is experienced in such matters.

We have a natural right to that true harmony that lies within ourselves. As explained in many different ways throughout this book, Mental Ataraxis is simply a pathway to the stillness that lies deep within each one of us.

There are few of us who are not aware of the natural harmony of the universe and few of us who are not, at some stage, a conscious witness to the perfect harmony all around us in nature; but all too few of us experience true harmony in ourselves. There are barriers built up by tension – barriers which we must transcend – and can through Mental Ataraxis – to reach that stillness where anxiety is gone and we can find the real wealth within ourselves.

EPILOGUE

We have talked of life, and many doubts have cleared from my mind. But it is only the doing of it that counts.

First let us guard and strengthen our body for it is the fortress in which we dwell, and from which we must fight.

Let us free our mind. Temper it with discipline, and enrich it with knowledge, for our mind is the essence of our being.

Calm comes to us. The calm and the stillness amid the clamour and the action. It is the calm of the spirit.

We understand beyond the constraints of logic, and our mind is free to range from the well-worn paths of the orthodox.

Secure when silence comes about us, yet rejoice in the company of our fellows, so that we need seek neither the solitude of the hills nor the merriment of the games and eating houses.

We work to contribute to the land of which we are part, and to maintain ourself that we may add to the well-being of those around us. And we enjoy the restorative power of leisure that we might do these things the better.

When love comes it purifies us, and in the act of love we transcend the earthly and so enhance our being.

Our mind is clear. We see the colour of it all and the meaning behind that which we see.

When we understand, there are no opposites. They have merged in the greater picture about us.

We know of pain and grief, but our mind is still and there is no hurt in it.

The seasons come and go. The planting, the ripening and the

harvest. The birth and growth and death. We feel the rhythm and the harmony of it all. And it is good.

And what of this other thing that comes in the eye of the storm and in the stillness of night, yet resides in a drop of dew? Cherish it, for it is born of the spirit and transcends all else.